TWAYNE'S WORLD AUTHORS SERIES

A Survey of the World's Literature

Sylvia E. Bowman, Indiana University

GENERAL EDITOR

SPAIN

Gerald Wade, Vanderbilt University
Janet W. Diaz, University of North Carolina at Chapel Hill

EDITORS

The Valencian Dramatists
of Spain's Golden Age

TWAS 371

The Valencian Dramatists
of
Spain's Golden Age

By JOHN G. WEIGER

University of Vermont

TWAYNE PUBLISHERS

A DIVISION OF G. K. HALL & CO., BOSTON

Library of Congress Cataloging in Publication Data
Weiger, John G.
    The Valencian dramatists of Spain's golden age.
    (Twayne's world authors series: Spain; TWAS 371)
    Bibliography: p. 157–66.
    Includes index.
    1. Spanish drama—Classical period, 1500–1700—History and criticism.
2. Spanish drama—Valencia—History and criticism. 3. Honor in litera-
ture.
    I. Title.
PQ6107.W4   1976   862'.3'09   75-25558
ISBN 0-8057-6219-1

To
BARBARA
who first toasted this book before the first
page was begun and who, throughout its
writing has stood by me amid all the tensions
and joys of deanship, scholarship and
friendship

Contents

About the Author

John George Weiger was born in Dresden, Germany and grew up in New York City. He did his undergraduate work at Middlebury College in Middlebury, Vermont, where he majored in Spanish. He received his M.A. from the University of Colorado in 1957. In 1966 he received the Doctor of Philosophy degree from Indiana University where he majored in Spanish, with minors in Portuguese and linguistics. Dr. Weiger has taught at the University of Colorado, Lawrence University, and since 1958, at the University of Vermont, where he is now Professor of Romance Languages as well as Dean of the College of Arts and Sciences.

Dr. Weiger's scholarly activities include papers delivered at the University of Kentucky Foreign Language Conference in 1968 on the *comedias* that Guillén de Castro adapted from the works of Cervantes, at the Modern Language Association in 1968 on the Valencian dramatist Tárrega, and in 1974, before the National Council of Teachers of English, on the relationship of Chaucer and a liberal arts education.

Dr. Weiger's publications beginning in 1958 include articles on Guillén de Castro, Virués, Tirso de Molina, Calderón, in journals such as the *Bulletin of the Comediantes, Hispanófila, Romance Notes*. He also wrote the introduction to the English translation of Castro's *The Youthful Deeds of the Cid*. He is currently at work on a book dealing with Cervantes.

Preface

There were three objectives in my mind as I began the writing of this volume. The most obvious is evident in the title, for it is indeed my purpose to acquaint the English-speaking reader with the nature of the drama of the last quarter of the sixteenth century in a region which boasted a well-developed culture, particularly in the drama. Secondly, by exploring the nature of that art, which flourished in the earlier part of what is called Spain's Golden Age, the period beginning roughly around the middle of the sixteenth century— although some would argue that it began with *La Celestina* in 1499—and ending during the last half of the seventeenth century. I wanted to point up what my own reading made very clear to me, namely, that most of the essential ingredients of what all the manuals of literature call the *comedia* as "created" by Lope de Vega (1562–1635), were already present in the works of his Valencian predecessors.

Since the honor concept is central to the entire body of literature known as the Spanish *comedia* of the Golden Age, I have attempted to focus on the contributions made to the development of this theme by the dramatists included in this study, that is, Artieda, Virués, Tárrega, Aguilar, Beneyto, Boil, and Turia. Although the Valencian dramatist who was closest to Lope, Guillén de Castro, is the most important and has been the subject of several articles of my own, I have not devoted a chapter to him, because William E. Wilson's recent book in Twayne's World Authors Series has dealt with the essential aspects of this poet. (See, however, my review of Wilson's book in the fall, 1974 issue of the *Bulletin of the Comediantes*.) The consideration of the honor concept, then, becomes my third purpose in writing this book, not merely to show its presence and to restate what has been said so often but to develop a thesis which has been brewing in my mind ever since I was first told to believe that there existed a dichotomy between inner and outer honor (virtue vs. reputation) or horizontal and vertical honor (inherited, innate honor vs. bestowed honor, i.e., again reputation). The final chapter, therefore, ties together the bits and pieces of the puzzle as garnered from a play-by-play analysis of the individual dramatists. My approach throughout the book has been to combine plot summaries with critical analysis and interpretation, rather than separate the two.

In presenting the dramatists, I have followed the order used by their modern editor, Eduardo Juliá Martínez, in his two-volume edition, *Poetas dramáticos valencianos*. With regard to translation, unless otherwise noted, all the translations from Spanish, French, and German are my own. I have tried to convey the sense and the imagery rather than attempt to imitate the rhyme, rhythm, or meter of the original. I am, of course, fully cognizant of the poetic *lacunae* that I leave in this manner, but my preference had to be the concepts, themes, motifs, and motivating forces.

I should like to thank Dr. Carlos Ortigoza, who first inspired me to follow this path; Dr. Walter Poesse, who kindly invited me to read, before the Modern Language Association in 1968, my paper "The Shadow of Death in the *Comedias* of Tárrega," which formed the nucleus of that theme as elaborated in chapter 4; Dr. Gerald Wade, who not only helped at points along the way, but whose initial encouragement gave me the needed impetus to proceed; finally, my family, whose patience in allowing "Dad" to be let alone was not only indispensable but remarkable.

JOHN G. WEIGER

Burlington, Vermont
January, 1975

Chronology

volume of a dozen *comedias*, this time by Tárrega, Aguilar, Turia, and Boil.

1617 Third and last visit of Lope de Vega to Valencia.

1623 Death of Aguilar.

1631 Death of Guillén de Castro.

1635 Death of Lope de Vega.

CHAPTER 1

The Valencian Dramatists:
An Introduction

I *The Valencian Academies: 1591–1616*

WITH the reading of the sonnet "In Praise of the Academy"
Bernardo Catalán de Valeriola assumed his post as president
of the newly founded *Academia de los Nocturnos* ("Academy of the
Nocturnals") at its inaugural session on October 4, 1591.[1] Although
prominent literary gatherings, or *tertulias literarias*, in Valencia
date back to the fifteenth century, the more formal academies have
their beginnings in the late sixteenth century with the *Academia de
los Nocturnos*. Joining as charter members were the dramatists[2]
Francisco Agustín Tárrega, Miguel Beneyto, and Gaspar de Aguilar.[3] Other dramatists joined later: Carlos Boil, Guillén de Castro
and Andrés Rey de Artieda, as well as Gaspar Mercader.[4]

Although Pérez de Guzmán asserts that the academy's influence
within the circles of the court apparently was nil,[5] Pfandl maintains
that the most renowned of all the academies was the illustrious
Academia de los Nocturnos of Valencia.[6] Sánchez qualifies his
evaluation by saying that this academy of men of letters is the most
important of the Spanish Golden Age outside Madrid and even then
there are very few in Madrid that surpass it.[7] Cotarelo y Mori agrees
that, without a doubt, the most important, or at least the best
known, among those outside Madrid is the *Academia de los Nocturnos* of Valencia,[8] and he concludes that among the most con-
spicuous *Nocturnos* are the poets of that famous Valencian group
which, around the end of the sixteenth century, succeeded in
counterbalancing the splendor and influence of the literature of
Madrid.[9]

Klein informs us that the members of the academy met each
Wednesday evening at the home of their president. At each session

a prose composition and poetic presentations were given.[10] As their name indicates, then, the members gathered nocturnally, using appropriately somber pseudonyms: *Silence, Fear, Shadow, Horror, Darkness, Secret, Obscurity, Danger, Fog,* and *Spy,* among others. Mérimée adds that the sessions were suspended each season for vacation between April and October.[11]

On April 13, 1594, after eighty-six sessions, the *Academia de los Nocturnos* concluded its third and final year of activity.[12] Guillén de Castro attempted to resurrect it in 1616 by founding the *Academia de los Montañeses del Parnaso* ("Academy of the Residents of Mount Parnassus"). Like its predecessor, the new academy was short-lived. No one seems to know, however, exactly when it was dissolved. Pfandl states that after the founding year of 1616 nothing further is known about this academy;[13] Mérimée writes that the academy died almost as soon as it was born (p. 552), and Juliá calls it the flower of one day.[14]

Sánchez remarks that not many details are known about the Parnassians but does venture to list Rey de Artieda and Tárrega among the members.[15] The former could not possibly have been a member, however, for he had died some three years earlier on November 16, 1613. La Barrera[16] and Martí Grajales[17] agree on this date, the latter critic having reproduced Artieda's death certificate.[18] Mérimée (p. 293) and Juliá[19] also agree that Artieda died in 1613.

With respect to Tárrega, it appears that he had died fourteen years prior to the founding of the Parnassus Academy. Martí Grajales,[20] Juliá (p. lxxiv), and Mérimée all agree that he died on February 7, 1602, Mérimée citing the burial registry (*Libre de sosterrars*), which is preserved in the archives of the cathedral (p. 460).[21]

Thanks to some verses included at the end of the epic poem *Los amantes de Teruel* (The Lovers of Teruel), we do know that its author, Juan Yagüe de Salas, was a member of the *Academia de los Montañeses del Parnaso.* Preceding the verses Yagüe writes: "Following the publication of this poem, the academy, newly resuscitated in the renowned city of Valencia by the well-known superior genius Guillén de Castro under the name of the *Montañeses del Parnaso,* asked me to summarize my poem without all of its episodes in the following octaves, which were read in the second meeting, I having been favored with admission to the academy with the pseudonym of Pindar."[22]

Mérimée informs us that Yagüe himself read the verses at the meeting of the academy, adding somewhat mischievously that the members undoubtedly must have appreciated their good fortune of being able to skip the reading of the complete work (p. 410). That Mérimée was not being entirely facetious is confirmed by the observation of Gascón y Guimbao, who states that Yagüe needed close to five hundred pages of hendecasyllabic lines, adding that he doubts very much that anyone has read them all.[23] Nonetheless, it should be noted in passing that Yagüe's poem was praised in sonnets by no less than Cervantes, Lope de Vega, and Valencia's own Guillén de Castro.

One other academy was founded during the years with which we are here concerned: the *Academia de los Adorantes* ("Academy of the Adorers"), under the leadership of the former *Nocturno*, Carlos Boil. As Sánchez points out, we barely know anything of this academy other than that it disappeared before 1600.[24]

The existence, or, more accurately, the function, of these academies served the intellectual and aesthetic hunger for sharing one's artistic endeavors with others of similar ambitions and abilities. Generally speaking, their *raison d'être* was analogous to that of professional guilds, fraternities, or clubs. The initiation rites, the ritual of assumed names, the membership requirements all lent legitimacy to the members' ultimate desire to have their own creations heard, read, and applauded.[25] Their rapid demise can be ascribed to the financial difficulties of maintaining such an establishment and to the disappearance of leading members as they either died or left for the lure of greater glories in Madrid or elsewhere.[26] Conversely, the rapidity with which one academy arose amid the ashes of another attests to the felt need for self-expression and peer approval.

Were they in fact peers? Did they have much in common? In subsequent chapters I shall deal with a common denominator: the *comedia*.

II *The Valencian "School"*

Ironically, it is precisely in the area of the *comedia* that all of the Valencians have been overshadowed by the four giants of this genre: Lope de Vega, Calderón de la Barca, Tirso de Molina, and Juan Ruiz de Alarcón. With the exception of Guillén de Castro, the Valencian dramatists are known today only to specialists in the field of the *comedia*. Even Castro is generally known only for one play, *Las*

mocedades del Cid (The Youthful Deeds of the Cid), and only a
relative handful of studies actually devote themselves to an analysis
of the work; the majority emphasize the fact that Castro's work
served as the source for Corneille's *Le Cid* and the beginnings of
French tragedy. Even more surprising, perhaps, is the fact that
prior to 1969, with the publication of the English translation of *The
Youthful Deeds of the Cid*, no English version of any play by any of
the Valencians, including Castro, was available. With regard to
book-length studies in English, only Sargent's 1930 volume on
Virués devoted an entire volume to any of the Valencians and we
have had to wait until 1973 for a book on Guillén de Castro.[27]

Nonetheless, nearly everyone who is familiar with Spanish literature seems to have heard of something called a "Valencian
School" of drama, often identified in some unexplained way with
Guillén de Castro, although the term "school" is rarely used by
established critics.[28] I have already cited Cotarelo y Mori's reference to the Valencians as a "group," a term repeated by Eduardo
Juliá Martínez, modern editor of all their works; a term employed
even earlier by Menéndez y Pelayo, who considered them to be
forerunners of the *comedia*.[29]

Valbuena Prat refers to the Valencians as a school that developed
independently of Lope de Vega, although the latter is described as
having given impetus to the Valencian theater which, in turn,
preserved various characteristics of the previous period of the
development of the Spanish drama.[30] On another occasion, Valbuena Prat felt that the Valencians were eventually drawn to Lope's
school as the result of his renovating influence,[31] an opinion shared
by Vossler who believed that one should rather speak of a Lopean
school than a Valencian one.[32]

Juliá, on the other hand, believes that Lope received much of his
early inspiration from the Valencians. Evidence of this is found in
Lope's *Belardo furioso*, which Juliá believes Lope wrote during his
Valencian days with a dash of realism but still abounding in touches
of surprise and marvel, elements common to the Valencian group.[33]

III   *The Honor Concept*

The honor code and its central role in the *comedia* of the Spanish
Golden Age has been described and analyzed so frequently that
recapitulation here seems superfluous. Its importance is sum-

marized in the oft-quoted observation that in hundreds and hundreds of Spanish dramas of the time, faith and honor are the "two rocks on which the whole ideological system of the *comedia* is built."[34] Its complexity is demonstrated in the following definition:

> Honour can mean the outward dignity
> conferred by rank; pride in the
> superiority of birth; public respect,
> the good name in which a family is held,
> and which is most easily damaged by any
> scandal touching its women. All this
> involves degrees of self-esteem.
> Honour can also mean integrity, and the
> recognition of integrity by the world
> at large. This is an idea which
> represents honour more as an expression
> of the moral worth of the individual,
> but it still implies public consent and
> is vulnerable to scandal and false report.
> The world at large is inclined to make
> easy snap-judgements and can impute
> dishonour by misunderstanding. The only
> defence against this oppressive force of
> opinion is an unrelenting watchfulness
> and a correspondingly arrogant self-assertion.[35]

That honor can be defined as more than a single concept is not, of course, peculiar to Spanish culture. In the Europe of the sixteenth and seventeenth centuries, Aristotle and Cicero were the classical authorities most often quoted on this matter:

> Honor to the orthodox Renaissance humanist,
> as to Aristotle and Cicero, had an outer form
> as well as an inner essence. In both senses
> honor was inseparably linked with virtue. In
> its inner aspect, honor was the love of
> virtue; in its outer it was the reward of virtue.[36]

Amezúa attempts to explain this dual aspect of honor in Spain by defining the Spanish word *honor* as an immanent attribute, intrinsic to man, while the other Spanish word *honra* is, he suggests, that same *honor* once it is publicly recognized by others.[37] I think that even in contemporary English this subtle distinction is felt when referring to someone as an *honorable* person, as distinguished from an act which someone carried out *with honor*. (The notion of "saving face" suggests the latter, i.e., external recognition, as opposed to an immanent quality, e.g., integrity.) Nonetheless, on reexamining all of these distinctions, it becomes increasingly difficult to distinguish between immanent attributes and their dependence upon external recognition. The well-known expression "virtue is its own reward," used and repeated since Antiquity, gives itself away by the very use of the word "reward," a concept which in its own right depends upon external recognition. No wonder, then, that as one pores over the *comedias* of the Spanish Golden Age, it becomes ever more nearly impossible to make substantive differentiation—aside from nuances—not only between the two words *honor* and *honra* but among a host of words which served as synonyms, such as the Spanish equivalents of "esteem," "fame," "reputation," "opinion," "name," "manhood," and the expressions "what (or who) I am," "what 'they' will say," etc.

The matter is made more complex by the fact that the adjectival forms of *honra* and *honor* are *honrado* and *honorado*. To say that someone is *honrado* is equivalent to saying that he possesses honor (either *honor* or *honra*). However, since the term *honorado* is rarely used in the *comedias*, it is a safe assumption that the linguistic coalescence of *honor* and *honra* into *honrado* contributed to the confusion not merely of words but of the concepts which they attempted to represent.

IV   *The Valencians' Place in the* Comedia

Around these concepts revolved the stuff of the Spanish *comedia* as woven by the man generally referred to as its creator, Lope de Vega, who himself advised that in the composition of a *comedia*, matters of honor were the best, since they move everyone forcefully.[38] Some of the Valencian playwrights were true contemporaries of Lope and thus serve only to point up contrasts or comparisons. On the other hand, the dramatists who formed part of the literary circle of Valencia (only Virués and Turia were not members of the *Academia de los Nocturnos*) include the author of the first Spanish play to bring a national legend to the stage (a favorite device of Lope's), a play which antedates Lope's first *comedia* by at least a decade (Artieda's *Los amantes*); the man (Virués) to whom Lope himself gave credit for the establishment of the three-act formula as well as for the blending of the comic with the tragic (both characteristics of Lope's *comedias*), as he admits in his treatise on how to compose plays;[39] the same man (Virués) who was the first to use the basic *romance* verse form in a *comedia (La infelice Marcela)*;[40] and, although he does not occupy a chapter to himself in this book, Guillén de Castro, the man who has been described as having given Spain the drama which, more than any other of the Golden Age, represents the tradition of the Spanish *comedia* by tying together the chivalresque traits of the Middle Ages, as expressed in the epics and the ballads known as *romances*, to the modern era, as evidenced by *The Youthful Deeds of the Cid.*[41] As Ebersole points out in his evaluation of the Valencian drama and the Valencian audiences, "the well-known *Academia de los Nocturnos*, very active around the end of the century, exerted a strong influence on the cultural life of the city and of the nation."[42]

These facts, added to Lope's own statements as well as his several visits to Valencia, indicate that a Valencian influence on him did indeed exist. Statements by respected critics as quoted earlier in this chapter, however, especially when bolstered by the following observation from no less an intellect than Américo Castro, prohibit a simple conclusion that the Valencian dramatists had a direct and patent influence on Lope: Américo Castro maintains that Lope *created* the literary genre appropriately called the national theater of Spain. He goes on to say that no matter how much we might wish to concede to his precursors, an abyss exists between them and Lope, adding that he, Américo Castro, believes it impossible to analyze Lope's theater by means of the elements brought along from the literary tradition of the sixteenth century.[43]

It appears, then, that the only fair conclusion to reach is that there existed a mutual influence between what is called the Lopean or national drama of Spain, that is, the *comedia*, and the Valencians who either barely preceded him or who were coetaneous with him.[44] The very use of words such as "precursors" and "brought along" (*aportados*) on the part of Américo Castro confirms that Lope as a dramatist did not appear spontaneously. I must agree with Froldi, who considers the commonly held view of a Lope de Vega springing up spontaneously and without direct ties to a continuing and evolving literary tradition to be a romantic dream (Froldi, pp. 12–16, especially note 5 on pp. 13–14). On the other hand, one cannot deny that it was Lope who brought the genre to fruition, that it was Lope who made it a truly *national* genre, that it was indeed the *comedia* of Lope de Vega.[45]

CHAPTER 2

Rey de Artieda

W ITH the author of *Los amantes* (The Lovers), we begin the study of the great tragic dramatists of the sixteenth century, choosing the word "great" with appropriate caution, as Hermenegildo observes; he adds that Artieda and Virués belong among the most typical and powerful representatives of that special type of tragedy which appeared in Spain in the 1580s.[1]

Micer Andrés Rey de Artieda, the "Sentinel" of the *Academia de los Nocturnos*, was born in Valencia in 1549.[2] He is, therefore, as Juliá suggests, the first of the authors who lived during the age in which the transformation of Valencian dramaturgy would be radical (p. xxiv). That Artieda himself was conscious of his position as precursor is seen in his prefatory verses to *The Lovers*, dedicated to D. Tomás de Vilanova, in which, after a brief summary of classical tragedy, he explains that the ancient style finally is coming to an end.[3] As Ebersole points out, although Artieda conceived *Los amantes* as a tragedy, his prefatory verses demonstrate a desire to compose a Hispanic work in opposition to classical demands. Among other things involving structure, Ebersole underscores the fact that Artieda's tragedy will have as its protagonists a man and a woman: no need for kings or gods, furies or centaurs.[4]

The Lovers, Artieda's only extant play, was first published in 1581, but in view of some lines from the above-mentioned prefatory verses, in which Artieda mentions having read Fr. Jerónimo Bermúdez' two *Nises* some months earlier, Mérimée concludes that *The Lovers* was composed no later than 1578.[5]

The legend of the lovers of Teruel has been the subject of a host of Spanish writers, notably Rey de Artieda, Yagüe de Salas, Tirso de Molina, Pérez de Montalbán, and Juan Eugenio Hartzenbusch, whose version is the best known.[6]

In Artieda's play, the lovers, known as Marcilla and Sigura, have been separated for a period of seven years, during which Sigura had

21

promised not to marry anyone else. Finding upon his return (only a few hours after the expiration of the waiting period) that Sigura has just married another man, Marcilla manages to hide in the new-lyweds' bedroom on their wedding night. After Sigura succeeds in persuading her husband (who, significantly, remains nameless throughout the drama) to respect her virginity one more day, Marcilla reveals his presence to Sigura and tries to kiss her. A monologue by Eufrasia, Sigura's cousin, reveals that Marcilla heaves a sigh and dies. Sigura and her husband take the body to the house of Marcilla's family. Marcilla's father finds the body and takes it to the church. Sigura laments the death of her lover and decides to go to the church and give him the coveted kiss. Once again by means of a monologue by Eufrasia, we next learn of the death of Sigura. Informed of what has occurred, the governor orders the lovers to be buried in the same sepulcher.

Unlike the many others who have concerned themselves with this legend, Artieda omits the name Teruel from the title of his work. According to Cotarelo, Artieda did this in order to emphasize the importance of the event rather than the location, it being of no significance whether it took place in Teruel or elsewhere.[7]

One of the reasons why Sigura had agreed to marry her husband was her fear that Marcilla might return famous and wealthy, scorn-ing her because her own estate would be small in comparison. Juliá observes that this touch on Artieda's part constitutes sharp psychological insight as he allows Sigura to fear that in the very attempt to accumulate wealth in order to satisfy the demands of her family to be rich enough to marry her, Marcilla could end up be-lieving himself superior to her and consequently scorn her (p. xliii). Mérimée also notes that Sigura's character displays a wealth of psychological observations (p. 311).

Hermenegildo, on the other hand, maintains that Artieda lacked the ability to penetrate the psychology of his characters. For Hermenegildo, Sigura turns out to be an unacceptable and defec-tively drawn character.[8] However, I find it difficult to accept Hermenegildo's conclusion, particularly since it is based on ob-servations such as his judgment that Sigura's demand that her husband respect her virginity after marriage represents an in-comprehensible attitude in view of her having denied Marcilla any right to have her fulfill the promises she had made to him prior to his departure.[9] Sigura's situation is somewhat more complex than Hermenegildo has observed.

In the first place, the fact that Sigura will not acquiesce to Marcilla's advances is easily explained by the fact that she is now married to another man, not to mention the awkward circumstances under which these advances are made, namely in her bridal bed with her husband asleep at her side. On the other hand, her refusal to yield to her husband's advances is as easily explained in view of the fact that her lifelong lover had returned that very day. Therefore, I do not find it very difficult to understand the "incomprehensible" attitude of the newlywed Sigura who had just seen her true love for the first time in seven years.

As mentioned above, the deaths of Marcilla and Sigura do not take place on stage but are related by the eavesdropping Eufrasia. Cotarelo concludes that this is due to the conception of theatrical decorum which Artieda entertained.[10] Mérimée, on the other hand, attributes this method to the fact that the deaths of the lovers are subordinate in significance to the emotions involved on the path to their death.[11]

The deaths of Marcilla and Sigura come as no surprise.[12] In the opening scene of the drama, Marcilla describes a dream he had, presaging the loss of Sigura (I, 3). The augury of misfortune is compounded when Marcilla calls for his sash and plumes, only to be given a black sash and yellow plumes instead of the red and white ones he requested, which, he is told, were lost at sea. Marcilla considers this incident related to his dream (I, 4).

In the very next scene, Sigura makes her first appearance by comparing the sound of a trumpet that is heard to the light which Hero watched go out,[13] adding quite explicitly that the trumpet is predicting her end (I, 5). Thus, the opening scenes of the drama presage the concluding ones.[14] Between these two points, Marcilla is involved in a conflict similar to that which some years later Guillén de Castro was to present in *The Youthful Deeds of the Cid*. Marcilla decides that it is better to act vigorously than calmly with regard to his having lost Sigura to another man, arguing that if he does not behave as a nobleman ought, "Am I to lose, for the sake of pleasing myself, the name which makes me be a man among men?" (I, 14).

This is an important place to pause for a detailed analysis, not only because the foregoing is of importance to this particular play but because of its significance in the development of the Spanish national drama. Marcilla's conflict goes far beyond that of a betrayed lover. His manhood is at stake, that manhood from which he derives his honor and, as a consequence, his very existence, symbolized by his name. As was pointed out in the previous chapter, the Spanish *comedia*, particularly as it is generally associated with Lope de Vega and later Calderón, revolved around the complex interweaving of the concepts represented by words such as "name," "reputation," "manhood," "being," among many others, all of them fusing into the generalized—and therefore more complex—concept of honor. If we are to consider, then, the place of Lope's Valencian forerunners in the development of what was to become the Lopean national drama, it seems clear that Marcilla's dilemma, his analysis of it, and its resolution in the hands of Artieda here in *The Lovers*, represents a precedent not only for the later Valencian drama by Guillén de Castro as suggested earlier but for the very essence of the *national* drama of Spain as made famous by Lope de Vega.

The eminent critic Américo Castro, in one of his last works, concluded that Lope de Vega provided new dimensions to the heroic caste as he conceived the structure of what Américo Castro calls "his" (Lope's) *comedia*. The renowned scholar goes on to observe that it was to be expected that Guillén de Castro, whom he labels Lope's disciple, could not portray Rodrigo, the hero of *The Youthful Deads of the Cid*, in situations other than those which bristled with conflicts. Rodrigo, he continues, must harmonize the unharmonizable: to kill his beloved's father without losing the sweetness of her love.[15] Yet here, some ten years before Lope de Vega's first *comedia* (not to mention the more than a quarter century which separates *The Lovers* from *The Youthful Deeds of the Cid*), Rey de Artieda presents a typically Lopean honor conflict, notwithstanding Américo Castro's repeated insistence that such a conflict was a problem of the expression of the honor feeling in the form of literature "initiated" by Lope de Vega.[16]

Marcilla's problem, then, to remain a man among men, is the dilemma presented by the possibility of not receiving the fulfillment of Sigura's promise to wait for him and preserve her love for him (the kiss), a result which would deprive him of his manhood and self-esteem (two forms of honor) and the equally unpleasant consequence that by having Sigura kiss him in her married state and in her bridal bed, Marcilla would be committing a dishonorable act. The kiss, then, becomes symbolic of Marcilla's manhood, which in turn is the basis of honor and existence. The denial of the kiss denies that basis and makes inevitable the death of Marcilla, who has lost his *raison d'être*.

When Marcilla's friend, Heredia, discovers the body, his only reaction is to ask who killed him.[17] The normal reaction on seeing a young hero dead is to conclude that *someone* killed him. Heredia's question, coupled with his own observation that Marcilla died in such a manner so that one cannot find the cause of death (I, 19) serves to emphasize the absence of that someone and causes us to concentrate on Marcilla himself. The key to these matters and, consequently, to the play itself, is provided in the eloquent eulogy of Marcilla's servant, Perafán, who is as well a poet and musician:

> But let my bitter voice come forth and break
> the terribly hard and stony entrails, for
> Death turned his glory into mourning
> and green ivy into funereal cypress.
> That it can be that the course of life be cut short and interrupted,
> just when a youth is in flower and thriving
> in the sweetest part of life,
> apparently without a blow and without a wound?
> These are Death's doings, but tyrannical ones,
> for against all laws she reaches out her arm,
> her natural prey being gray hair,
> where Nature is more likely to be offended.
> Death, if for the sake of showing yourself to be impartial,
> you level all ages and conditions, be aware
> that although you equate the poor with the rich,
> you err in shortening life so much.
> All that is born under the sun is subject
> to dying, but I don't doubt that Nature is
> displeased to see it not reach the end it could have;
> . . . .
> But I am consoled and assuaged in part that that
> faith you have in the infidels and which you show them,
> will not erase in Mauritania and Lybia
> what his famous right arm accomplished;
> for what you turn into ashes,
> Fame revives and immortalizes.
>
> (I, 18–19)

Hermenegildo, who limits his comments to the first octave of Perafán's monologue, interprets this passage to mean simply that life may be cut short without warning and that man can never understand the reasons behind it.[18] That is, of course, accurate but far from complete. Perafán is indeed lamenting that life may be cut

short, but rather than focus on the surprise element or its in-
comprehensibility, his concern in the first octave revolves around
the death of *youth* and that this could happen without a battle. In
short, the reaction suggested by Heredia's earlier comment. In
addition, this first octave describes the power of Death to convert
the green ivy of youth into the cypress, symbol of the funereal.

The second octave continues the theme of the death of youth,
together with the traditional concept of Death as the equalizer of
men. Perafán chides Death for her exaggeration of impartiality, for
whereas it is acceptable to kill the wealthy as well as the poor, Death
is overstepping her obligations when she shortens the life of youth,
for death among the young is contrary to the laws of Nature, a theme
which is continued in the following stanza.

The final stanza is the most important for the matter at hand.
Having accused Death of being in league with the Moslem infidels,
Perafán finds consolation in the fact that neither the Moors nor Death
can erase the deeds of Marcilla. In other words, Death does not ex-
punge what man has made of himself during his stay on earth, for
Fame revives it and makes it eternal.[19] Thus Fame has the power to
triumph over Death, a concept previously introduced by Artieda in
the prefatory verses to this play (I, xxvii). This is not a new concept for
postmedieval man, but as a central function in the Spanish drama,
particularly as related to the honor concept, its appearance here in
The Lovers is significant.

As a dramatic motif, the importance of fame appears early in the
sixteenth century in Torres Naharro's *Himenea*, in which it is advised
that for the sake of fame, life is worth losing.[20] At first blush it would
seem that such a statement is a paradox and might better be expressed
by suggesting that for the sake of fame life is worth *living*, since fame
is generally regarded as the consequence of notable accomplishments. However, as students of this period know, fame was not so
simply interpreted. In addition to this self-evident definition of fame
and how it enhanced one's life, the relationship among fame, life,
death and honor is best described in the famous "Coplas por la
muerte de su padre" (Verses on the Occasion of the Death of His
Father), by the fifteenth-century poet Jorge Manrique. Translated
freely, Manrique addresses his dead father as follows:

> Let not the frightful battle which you await
> be a bitter one for you, for you leave

> behind you here another and longer life
> of fame. Although this life of honor is not
> eternal or real either, it is nonetheless
> much better than the other mortal,
> temporal one. . . . And with this confi-
> dence and with the absolute faith that
> you possess, leave us with firm hope
> of achieving that other third life.[21]

The significance of this passage cannot be overemphasized. Manrique suggests that there are *three* forms of life. The first (and of least importance) is the mortal, temporal life equivalent to our physical stay on earth. More important is "another and longer life of fame," which he also calls a "life of honor," a life which is not ever-lasting either but which not only endures beyond the life of the body, but is, more importantly, a *better* life. Finally, of course, there is the most important variety of all, "that other third life," by which he means the eternal life of the soul.

It is the intermediate variety, that "longer life of fame," that better "life of honor," which is of importance to the drama. This is the life we leave behind us here on earth, a life dependent upon fame and honor, hence dependent on what we have been able to make others think of us. Since this is a better life, it is easy to understand the quotation from Torres Naharro to the effect that for the sake of fame, life is worth losing, since it means that for the sake of a better and more enduring life, the lesser, physical life is worth giving up. This other life, then, this better life of fame and honor which outlives us, or, put metaphorically, this other life in whose form we continue to live on, is the basis upon which so much of the honor concept rests.

However, one does not achieve this form of life without having earned it: that is, one's physical life must provide the basis for that better life of honor by conducting oneself as befits a man who prizes his honor and reputation. Since the demonstration of manliness is one of these ways, it follows that to lose one's image of manliness (the Spaniards use the words *machez, machismo* and *hombria*)[22] is to lose one's basis for existence.

In *The Lovers,* Marcilla lost his reason for living when he lost his *hombría* through the denial of the kiss. Sigura at first fails to understand this as she marvels that Marcilla should die for the sake of a kiss, something which she calls a light matter, despite Marcilla's earlier opinion that "it is a weighty matter, for although what I'm asking for appears to be little, who dares to give a kiss gives us a great deal" (I, 15). Sigura does finally comprehend as she explains that her resistance and opposition "lasted while you were a man; but now that you are one no longer, let my resistance end. I shall give you the kiss" (I, 21). Thus it is that she kisses the dead Marcilla and dies herself. The drama ends with the lovers destined to be buried jointly. The final words of the play proper are spoken by Heredia: "Who would imagine that the one to unite them should be the one who separates everything?" (I, 24), an obvious reference to Death.

Sigura's kiss has restored Marcilla's *hombría* and hence his fame, assuring him of that other more glorious life of honor. Marcilla's own question ("Am I to lose . . . the name which makes me be a man among men?"), which we now can understand in its multiple ramifications, is answered in the negative by Fame in the epilogue:

> Although Fate triumphs on the Final Day,
> he who was something in life, will be so dead,
> if his worth is publicized by me
> ·
> Marcilla, therefore, is today the same he has been,
> and Sigura after him, since I name her.
>
>   (I, 24)

Thus Fame personified explains that, although there is yet to come a final Day of Judgment, if someone was something in life, [23] he will be something in death, provided that Fame mentions him and his accomplishments. Having named both Marcilla and Sigura, therefore, Fame assures them of that life of fame.

Sigura's husband, on the other hand, has remained nameless (i.e., fameless) throughout the drama. Informed of what has occurred, he does nothing, claiming that neither has Marcilla wronged him nor has Sigura by kissing a dead man, ignoring the reproof of his cousin, who tells him to get out of his house, calling him a man not worthy of the name. Since he prefers to overlook his dishonor and thereby fails to demonstrate his *hombría* (which is why his cousin accuses him of being unworthy of the name *hombre*), the husband does not achieve a life of honor and fame after death, a result made clear by the final words of Fame: "What I have never done with a man, I do, if you notice, with the husband, for being what I am, I keep his name silent" (I, 24).

In earlier pages of this chapter, I have tried to show that many of the basic ingredients which were to become the hallmarks of what is called

Lope de Vega's national drama of Spain are already present in this, the only extant play by his Valencian predecessor, Rey de Artieda. Furthermore, I believe I have shown that not only are the seeds of the national *comedia* present in *The Lovers* (some of which had their germination even earlier), but the fundamental aspects of the honor concept—it is obviously too soon to speak of an honor *code*, and we may have to go beyond Lope and wait for Calderón to codify it— are logically and patently developed as the thread of a drama whose plot is not original with Artieda. In my mind, then, there can be no doubt that Artieda was in spirit a forerunner of Lope de Vega. How much he was simply an antecedent and how much he served as a direct influence remains uncertain. That he anticipated Lope in matters of central importance to the *comedia* cannot be doubted.

Perhaps it was with similar thoughts in mind that Juliá unequivocally concluded that among the Valencians only Guillén de Castro succeeded in surpassing Artieda.[24] The most evenhanded assessment of this play and what we can learn of its author is probably that by Crawford, who observes that "the originality of Rey de Artieda does not lie . . . in the invention of the plot and in the arrangement of dramatic situations, but in his choice of a story replete with romantic incidents. . . . The earlier Spanish drama offers us no serious portrayal of love with its fatal consequences when thwarted. Here is represented the painful conflict between duty and will in the lady's heart, and the grief of the lovers, gradually intensified throughout the four acts. . . . In *Los amantes* emphasis is laid upon the crisis, and our sympathy is awakened by the moral struggle of the lovers against fatality."[25]

Finally, although I have been emphasizing the place of Artieda's work on the path to the Lopean drama, the interested reader may wish to compare it with the version of that other giant of the *comedia*, Lope's contemporary, Tirso de Molina, who titled his work *Los amantes de Teruel*. Tirso's contributions have been described elsewhere.[26] More significant, perhaps, with regard to the Valencians' contributions to the national drama and Artieda's place in that evolution, is the fact that as recently as the 1960s, despite the erudition of Mérimée, Juliá, Froldi, and others, major scholars continue to be ignorant of the Valencians' works.

Thus, Aubrun, who had reduced the total worth of what he calls the Valencian School to Guillén de Castro's having grafted onto the budding *comedia* cuttings from the Italian drama,[27] says of the seventeenth-century *Los amantes de Teruel* by Montalbán that in the latter's version, "perhaps" for the first time in the Spanish theater, money becomes the motivating force for the action. Yet not only has Artieda anticipated him in this aspect but in the far more important elements suggested by Aubrun, according to whom Montalbán "inaugurates" what the French scholar calls a new literary technique: the race against time, fatal passion, the cruel destiny of the protagonists, and immoderate use of asides. All of these, claims Aubrun, are the "original ingredients" of Montalbán's work and will spice the dramatic and novelesque genres for centuries.[28] Clearly all of these contributions are to be credited to Valencia's Artieda.

As Ruiz Ramón has observed, *Los amantes* represents a step forward in the Spanish theater, a step which clears the way toward "the conquest of our theater of the Golden Age."[29] In *The Lovers*, then, Rey de Artieda sets the tone of what is to follow, defining without undue elaboration the components of honor and fame as they relate to life and death, concepts which will become more complex in the hands of the subject of the following chapter, Virués.

CHAPTER 3

Virués

ALL those who have dealt with Virués lament the paucity of biographical data.[1] Captain Cristóbal de Virués was born in Valencia, probably around 1550, and, although several scholars cite 1609 as the year of his death, he was probably still alive in 1614.[2] Primarily a soldier, Virués spent the greater part of his life away from Valencia, which explains why he was not a member of the *Academia de los Nocturnos*.[3]

Juliá writes that Virués, even though he might not be within the mainstream of his time, was one of those who wielded the greatest influence upon his contemporaries (p. xlvi). Nowadays, however, Virués' chief claim to fame in the drama[4] appears to be limited to the reference which Lope de Vega made to him in his *New Art of Composing Plays in These Times*, crediting Virués with the establishment of the three-act formula for the *comedia*.[5] Scholars have generally considered Virués' position in the development of the Spanish drama as that of precursor to Lope. The most significant study in this respect is that of Atkinson, who considers Virués as the halfway mark between Seneca and Lope.[6] Atkinson mentions Lope's reference to Virués in the *New Art* but goes on to say that "much more significance attaches, however, to his other tribute in *El Laurel de Apolo*, 1630 :

> ¡O ingenio singular! en paz reposa,
> a quien las Musas Cómicas debieron
> los mejores principios que tuvieron
> Celebradas Tragedias escribiste.

> [Oh unique genius! rest in peace,
> to whom the Comic Muses owed
> the best principles they owned.
> You wrote Celebrated Tragedies.]

. . . [which] would make of Virués the true founder of the Spanish national drama."[7] With respect to the two alternatives for the use of versification, namely, conformity with the character of the speaker or conformity with the character of the situation, Virués chose the latter, "and once more Lope was to follow suit." Finally, Atkinson points out that Virués tended more and more to make his tragedies turn on amorous passion and intrigue "and again Lope had but to take over where the Valencian left off."[9]

Nearly every scholar concerned with the dramatic art of Virués has made mention of the difference between Virués *Elisa Dido* and his four other plays.[10] *Elisa Dido* is written in five acts, makes use of a chorus, excludes comic elements, and is, in Crawford's judgment, the only "other tragedy definitely based upon classical models . . . written in Spain during the sixteenth century. . . ."[11] Virués' other plays are written in three acts, do not use a chorus, and are tragicomic in substance.[12] There exists another difference of some importance which I wish to bring out, namely, that, although all five of Virués' dramas demonstrate a didactic intent, the last four plays are exemplary only by providing examples of what one must *not* imitate, or, as I shall show shortly, didacticism "by opposite example." In *Elisa Dido,* on the other hand, Virués presents a model to be imitated.

I   Elisa Dido

As one might expect in a drama based on classical models, fate is an important element of *Elisa Dido*. Dido herself defines it:

> Fate, which is a divine disposer
> which, by secret ways not understood
> by human knowledge, leads men to
> certain ends for which they were
> put in the world by the great
> Maker of men and world.
>
> (I, 146–47)

But the course of man's destiny is not irreversible, provided it is tempered by divine grace.[13] As the chorus points out, "if Heaven has no pity for man, then man is without remedy and without consolation" (I, 153). Consequently, those who lose faith and hope are themselves lost. Hence the death of Seleuco, who had declared that "the die is cast" (I, 154), disillusioned by the inconstancy of hope: "What can I do? What good are you, Hope, since you go around giving and taking?" (I,

156). Carquedonio, who died together with Seleuco, also had given up hope, saying that "the ordinary course of the world wants no one to be able to be happy" (I, 159).

Similarly, Ismeria's fate is not only to lose her lover, Seleuco, but her position as Dido's confidante as well. Her punishment is likewise the result of her loss of faith:

> What is there without deceit in this world?
> What is there without pain in this life?
> Woe on him who trusts things of the world!
> Woe on him who puts faith in things of the earth!
> Deception is this whole decrepit world;
> Pain is this whole decrepit life!
>
> (I, 155)[14]

The frustration of Iarbas' plans similarly is caused by his loss of hope: "Oh, false hopes of the earth," he exclaims, as he describes life in this "miserable world" (I, 177).

Dido, on the other hand, is a firm believer in the use of one's free will. She considers unacceptable Iarbas' demand that she marry him or face war not merely because of her vow of chastity but because "the matter must depend on free will" (I, 147).[15] The world is for Dido a "bitter war" (I, 161). Hence all that is needed for her mission to be successful is divine grace. Dido's mission, I must stress, is the salvation of her people. The preservation of her chastity, then, becomes more symbolic than real, a point of view almost reached by Sargent, who considers the people's salvation and Dido's chastity on the same level:

> Far from being the love-lorn widow who . . . de-
> stroyed herself in a passion of ungovernable de-
> spair, the Dido of Virués is a prudent queen who,
> motivated by devotion to the dead Siqueo and ris-
> ing Carthage, outwitted a too insistent suitor by
> a noble self-sacrifice which at once protected
> her people and saved her self-esteem.[16]

Logic indicates, however, that the salvation of the people and the chastity of Dido cannot be considered on the same level.

Were the salvation of the people her only consideration, Dido could merely have accepted Iarbas' demand, as indeed she pretends to do. On the other hand, were her chastity her only consideration, she could refuse Iarbas' proposition and fight. If the dilemma were to end here, I would have to accept Sargent's equation of the two desires. But what assurance does Dido have that Iarbas will respect her last request, namely, that he give liberty to her people after her death? Logic supplies no answer. Evidently the preservation of her chastity through death holds a greater value than her "self-esteem," a symbolic value which, far from being a mere corollary to the people's salvation, *represents* that salvation. Pirro, one of Dido's captains, understands this well as he decries Dido's apparent acquiescence to Iarbas' demands, believing that Dido's honor, which up to this point she had so strictly maintained, is now at stake: "She is damning herself by giving herself to a barbarian; and we similarly are being damned" (I, 153).

The notion that Iarbas is a barbarian (despite the apparently pagan background of the entire play)[17] is repeatedly uttered by nearly every member of the cast. Carquedonio refers to him as "this arrogant barbarian" (I, 152); Clenardo laments the possible marriage of Dido to "her enemy, a crude barbarian" (I, 167); Ismeria calls him "this barbarian king of Mauritania" (I, 169); and Seleuco provides the appropriate perspective for this shared view of Iarbas as a barbarian by speaking of the "infamous marriage" (I, 153).

This emphasis on Iarbas' status as a barbarian within the context of a marriage which would remove fame (hence remove honor) provides the necessary contrast so that Dido may stand out as someone worthy of the honor and fame which may lead to another life as described in chapter 2. In contrast to the frequent reference to Iarbas as a barbarian, then, there emerges a series of suggestions that Dido is in Heaven's favor. In fact, all her thoughts and deeds are the result of the advice of her dead husband, Siqueo, who had received special dispensation to return after his death (I, 150), whereupon Dido promised to obey the "order which on Heaven's behalf you brought me" (I, 158), specifically explained later as Dido's having promised to Siqueo chastity ever since that moment (I, 176).

Dido's goal is "'for peace, for holy peace" (I, 147) and, as the drama progresses, we are informed that her "spirit is divine" (I, 168), along with Delbora's prophetic wish that "Heaven allow her to prosper and provide her with glorious death and eternal, illustrious fame" (I, 169). The relationship between these words and those of Jorge Manrique as discussed in the previous chapter is evident. Consequently, when Dido commits suicide in order to "attain the great victory which I achieve with my death," even Iarbas is forced to admit that "divine chastity has been the cause of your early, bitter death" (I, 176). Not only does he comply with Dido's request to free her people, but now he, too, understands, proclaiming that Dido be considered "goddess of Carthage, eternally with sacred worship, honor and reverence" (I, 177), a request which is promptly respected by the people.[18]

In *Elisa Dido*, then, Virués presents an easily discernible picture of the three kinds of life as defined a century earlier by Jorge Manrique. The first or physical life of the soul in the body is described as a struggle, painful and full of illusion. Despite this, a life which is lived to preserve honor and fame provides, through a "glorious" death, that longer and better life of fame, a life achieved by Dido. As for the third and eternal life, Siqueo's return visit from the dead described it as the soul's enjoyment of eternal and celestial repose.

II   La Gran Semíramis

Virués' next drama, *La gran Semíramis* (Great Semíramis), presents another case of suicide in the very first act.[19] Menón, general of Nino's forces, leaves the battlefield to greet his wife Semíramis: "And although, by coming here, I risk my honor, whoever judges me will see, if it does defame me, that it matters more to enjoy you, my heaven, than all the glory the earth can give me" (I, 26).[20] The opening lines of the play thus present Menón on the road to self-extinction, despite his awareness of the importance of "honor, which is the prime possession" (I, 29).[21]

Nino, the king, falls in love with Semíramis and asks Menón to give her to him in exchange for his daughter, pointing out that "being your king, I am asking for what I can have by virtue of my power" (I, 32). Menón refuses, saying that even if the eternal fire were to burn him and "although I were to turn into a nonbeing, which is a greater discredit, my tongue could never say yes to that" (I, 32). Nino takes Semíramis anyway, leaving Menón no choice but suicide: "Tired and sad life, . . . don't offer resistance, . . . leave your residence to the healer of people, to sweet, sweet death" (I, 33).

Rey de Artieda had referred to Death as the one "who separates everything." For Virués she is "the healer of people," a sweet Death who merely replaces life in the residence of the human body. Here, as in *Elisa Dido*, there is no victory *over* death but triumph *through* death, a triumph over the other and worse possibility: to become a nonentity ("a nonbeing, which is a greater discredit"). Man has two alternatives open to him: to die (i.e., physically but with honor) and to cease to exist (i.e., to be without honor and hence not to be). We see again, then, that honor is the basis of existence.

The death of Nino in the second act is suicide only when seen from one point of view. After getting Nino to agree to letting her rule the kingdom for five days, Semíramis assumes the clothes of Ninias, son of Semíramis and Nino, and has Ninias don her robes and stay with the Vestal Virgins. (The success of this impersonation is explained by the repeated references to the nearly identical features of mother and son.) After imprisoning Nino, Semíramis has him brought before her. Thinking that she is Ninias, Nino assumes that the son has killed the mother. Semíramis allows him to believe this, whereupon Nino wishes to commit suicide and is given a glass of poison which he accepts willingly. Thereupon he is informed of the true state of affairs and despite a frantic call for an antidote, Nino dies.

As for the death of Semíramis herself, Virués, in the manner of Artieda, does not present the death scene on stage but has it related by the snooping Diarco, who had witnessed the murder of Semíramis.[22]

It seems clear from the beginning that Semíramis must die.[23] Her sins run the gamut from acquiescence to Nino's proposal to trade her for his daughter (act I), through murder of her second husband (act II), lasciviousness (acts II and III) to incest (act III). One might wish to argue that the murder of Nino is simply revenge for her abduction. Mérimée (p. 344), for instance, considers that the second act shows us the revenge of virtue over passion. However, sixteen years have passed since Semíramis' abduction, sixteen years during which she herself says that her captivity has ruled in her with the title of queen without being queen (I, 39). As Mérimée himself points out, Semíramis barely objected to her abduction, accompanying her ravisher after a timid protest of three words! In short, through her behavior and through her words, Semíramis' objective has been to gain control of power.

Although I have referred to Nino's poisoning as murder, one must bear in mind that though he was lured into the trap by Semíramis' machinations, Nino takes the poison willingly. It is significant, then, that just as Menón had been unable to castigate Nino, since the latter as king was the source of honor and hence unpunishable, so now only Nino himself is able to administer his own punishment.[24]

Lasciviousness on the part of Semíramis is repeatedly pointed out. Semíramis herself, referring to Zopiro, the servant, tells us that she is determined to seduce him, considering such lovemaking her recreation (I, 38). Later, wearing her son's clothing, she says that her identity will only be known by "the one who undresses me, and that will be Zopiro" (I, 45). After her death, we learn that Semíramis had killed "more than a thousand young men with whom she satisfied her blind appetite, seducing each one in a single night or a single day in her lascivious bed" (I, 53).

Although Semíramis' incestuous desires are not permitted to be realized because of her death, her feelings are made extremely clear. When Ninias tells her that he is proud to be her son, Semíramis murmurs that this makes her sad and deprives her of all the delight "which your heavenly beauty can give" (I, 47). When he calls her "beloved mother," she delights in the first word but "how sour is the word 'mother,' which you put with it" (I, 48). The disgust which Ninias feels—and not his desire to avenge his father's death[25]—sets in motion his urge to kill Semíramis, despite some momentary moral vacillation: "Who would give death to the one who gave him life?" (I, 48).

An important aspect of Semíramis' character must be taken into consideration. It is evident that Virués, as many of the Valencians who were to follow, liked to portray virile women whose intriguing and underhanded ways lead men to their destruction. Sargent suspects an autobiographical element in this: "There is nothing to indicate that Virués ever married. Did personal experience lead him to picture his heroes dupes of unscrupulous women?"[26] It is significant, then, that Semíramis executes every act while clothed as a man.

In the opening scene of the play, in which Menón deserts the battlefield to greet Semíramis, the latter is clothed as a man, ostensibly because of the bellicose surroundings. However, the masculine attire also causes her virility to stand out, as she immediately proceeds to devise a plan of warfare which is successfully carried out by the soldiers. This is what causes Nino to fix his attention upon her and subsequently "abduct" her while she is still clothed as a man. In short, both of her husbands have been portrayed as unable to resist her while she was in masculine attire.

In the second act, Semíramis achieves the "suicide" of Nino by appearing before him as their son, that is, as a man. The obvious need for this has already been pointed out. Nevertheless, she does not remove her manly attire but continues to pose as her son for the next six years![27] It is during these years that she has led Zopiro and the countless other young men first to her bed and subsequently to their death. It appears that Semíramis has begun to enjoy her virility, for although it must be clear to the "more than a thousand young men" that her feminine charms are attractive, Semíramis herself has become enamored of her *masculine* qualities.

Finally dressed as herself once more, she falls in love with her son, who now is dressed as Semíramis had been—that is, the "masculine" Semíramis of the past six years—and who looks exactly like her (I,47). In other words, the perversity which has been noted by many scholars is not so much incest as narcissism. She has really fallen in love with her own masculine image.

After killing Semíramis, Ninias tries to convince the people that she ascended to Heaven in the form of a dove (I, 56). This is in sharp contrast not only with the true facts of her death but also with the facts of her life, her true ancestry having been revealed only moments before: Semíramis was in fact the daughter of a "vile and lowly man" and a prostitute (I, 54).

Sargent observes that "in this play Virués presents not only the rise and fall of a great queen, but the effect of it upon the people she ruled."[28] This at once brings to mind *Elisa Dido*. As I have shown earlier, Dido's death brings peace to her people and the long-lasting variety of life or fame to herself. Semíramis' death is painted in similar fashion by Ninias, but the effect is voided by the prior revelation of Semíramis' origin, by the description of her actual death, and by Zelabo and Diarco, who (in asides) interrupt Ninias' fabricated eulogy to comment on its mendacity: "These are the deceptions of men!" (I, 56).

Sargent claims that "Dido's case is unique,"[29] but it is not so when one bears in mind what I have previously pointed out, namely, that in *Elisa Dido*, Virués presents a model of moral virtue to be imitated, whereas in the remaining dramas, beginning with *Great Semíramis*, the examples offered are not to be followed.[30] The deaths of the two queens do not contradict but complement each other. Dido's death converts her into a goddess; Ninias attempts to do the same with Semíramis (for selfish reasons) and fails. Both women displayed manly characteristics related to the concept of fame and that glorious life of honor after physical death, a concept explained in relatively traditional terms in chapter 2 of this book and explored further in the final chapter. In addition, there exists another form of honor which is innate in the noble; Zelabo's revelation of Semíramis' origins deprives her of that sort of honor as well.[31]

It would appear, then, that Virués censures the woman who becomes enamored of her own virility and thence sets forth to make fools of men.[32] It is well to bear in mind that, although the device of the woman dressed as a man was a commonplace in the *comedia*,[33] such an act could be interpreted as a mortal sin if the woman's motive was other than self-preservation or sheer frivolity.[34] The question of sin does not apply to *Great Semíramis*, of course, since Christian awareness is entirely absent. Menón, for example, displayed no cognizance of the Christian attitude toward suicide. Nevertheless, Virués' portrayal of the abuse of masculine prerogatives is patent in his characterization of Semíramis, whose appearance in male attire during the major portion of the play could not have failed to have its effect upon the audience of those times. In a forthcoming article announced in the 1973 edition of his book and which, at this writing, I have not yet seen, Hermenegildo promises an explanation of Virués' portrayal of women as "monstrously ambitious" and who "initiate authentic mortal convulsions in the royal courts where they reside; [the findings] clarify as well the presence of women who go about in the guise of men . . . or who manipulate various men for the realization of their plans."[35]

III   Atila Furioso

Another unscrupulous woman spends a good part of her life in male attire in *Atila furioso* (Furious Atila). Flaminia is having a romance with King Atila, who has installed her as a page in the palace, not only to disguise her sex from the queen (who, incidentally, falls in love with "Flaminio"), but because Atila enjoys seeing Flaminia as a man (I, 97). Hermenegildo wonders whether there is a homosexual interest here, an interest which he finds inexplicable in view of Atila's unbridled desire for women, and thus concludes that Virués did not hit the mark in his characterization of Atila.[36]

I must agree that the characterization of Atila is not a convincing one. It appears that in the figure of Atila, Virués let his didacticism by opposite example run away with him. Wishing to point out the qualities that can engender an evil monarch, Virués combined them all in one figure who, rather than being a person, is a personification—nay, a caricature—of all those evil qualities at once: infidelity, inclemency, lust, murder, and madness.

Doubtless it was this play, and the character of Atila in particular, that led Atkinson to observe that the attempt to heighten tragic effect by the mere accumulation of horrors must ultimately defeat its own ends "by debasing the stuff of tragedy until it becomes laughable."[37] Earlier, Schaeffer refused to summarize some of Virués' plays because of their wealth of murders and other horrors, explaining that he wished to spare his readers the plot summaries.[38] Crawford's earlier edition of his previously cited *Spanish Drama Before Lope de Vega* concluded that "in order to strengthen the force of his moral lesson, [Virués] deals with crime on a heroic scale, of such extravagant proportions that the reader of today, instead of trembling at the consequences of misdoing, merely smiles incredulously." The latest edition of Crawford's work no longer includes that sentence, limiting its interpretive comment to the observation that "delirium reaches its limit in *Atila furioso*."[39]

Froldi dismisses *Furious Atila* by saying that just thinking of the beginning is enough and after a hurried description of the entangled love relationships, drops further discussion of the play with an exclamation point. On the other hand, one scholar has seen a glimmer of purpose amid all the madness. Flecniakoska has suggested that Virués' taste for horror is not gratuitous for it corresponds to a desire for moral didacticism.[40] It is significant, then, that this monster, Atila,[41] understands the concept of honor as he himself describes it in his first appearance in the drama:

> He whose valor is not offended by insult
> should not be given among men the name of man:
> he whose valor is not incensed by insult
> should not be called among men man;
> he who intends, without avenging insult,
> to achieve among men renown,
> does not have a forehead worthy of a crown,
> nor does his person merit any respect.
> I feel so strongly any small insult
> that I am, until I have avenged myself,
> burning in flames.

(I, 95)

Such a conception of honor is by no means uncommon in the Spanish theater of the sixteenth and seventeenth centuries and recalls Marcilla's concern in Artieda's *The Lovers* for the preservation of "the name which makes me be a man among men." In a word, Atila's conception of honor is based upon being a man, upon his *hombría*, the manifestation of which is the vengeance of an affront, no matter how minor the insult may be. Yet, Virués chooses as the exponent of this conception an ogre whose own description of himself is as follows:

> I'm a hungry lion, I'm a horrendous tiger,
> I'm a vicious crocodile and fierce dragon,
> frightful ghost, monster and specter.
> I'm astounding thunder, wondrous lightning,
> earthquake, grate, horror and havoc.
> I'm more than this: man of this century.
>
> (I, 112–13).

Ricardo, his aide, observes, "Madmen and children speak truths."

This monster, this "man of this century," proceeds to do what countless other husbands in other *comedias* find themselves obligated to do: informed that his wife is receiving visits from another man, Atila kills her. The significant fact, however, is that Virués has selected the incarnation of iniquity and madness for this role.

It appears, then, that in the characterization of Atila, Virués frowns upon that aspect of the honor code which not only permits but requires a husband to kill an unfaithful wife. This is a reflection of a polemic which raged in the sixteenth century concerning the contradictory tenets of the honor code and Christianity. The literature on this subject is vast, but it has been summarized in a concise manner by Otis Green, who cites Azpilcueta to the effect that, since it is admissible for a man to kill in the defense of his property, it is therefore acceptable for him to kill in the defense of his honor because honor is more valuable than property. Azpilcueta adds, however, "that the husband who kills or wishes to kill his wife having found her in adultery, sins mortally, although by law he receive no punishment therefor."[42]

Green further quotes from Antonio de Torquemada's *Coloquios satíricos*, in which it is stated that "we must consider honor in one of two ways. One of these ways is *as Christians* [italics added by

Green] . . . . That being so, what is there today so contrary to the
true Christian faith as honor?"[43] Thus, according to the two quotations above and emphasized by Green's italics, the concept of
honor as based not upon one's moral worth but upon the actions of
another whose truancy deprives one of one's honor is inconsistent
with Christian philosophy. It is significant, therefore, that Virués
selected for this role a man whose reputation in history is that of the
Antichrist, the scourge of God.[44]

Thus it is that for the immoral Atila, death is not the welcome
healer as was the case for Menón, but the means to extinction.
Poisoned by Flaminia, Atila thinks she is Death and wishes to kill
her (i.e., to kill Death):

> But now, my unfaithful Death,
> now I see who is destroying me.
> . . . .
> I've got hold of you well, well;
> Death, my wild enemy!
> . . . .
> Come, Death, for it's to the deep abyss
> that I shall drag you with me,
> . . . .
> Come, come, run; come with me.
> Follow me, Death, you traitor.
>
> (I, 115)

Atila kills Flaminia as he himself falls dead, having reached "the
extreme point of eternal misery" (I, 116). The lament which Virués
puts in the mouth of the servant Ricardo contrasts sharply with
Perafán's lament in *The Lovers* and leaves no room for doubt with
respect to the kind of exemplarity personified in Atila:

> Oh well-deserved death,
> how you shall be of his life
> clear example and testimony!
> . . . .
> Oh just payment and punishment,
> and just Hell to which you go,
> for you were of Satan
> such a great follower and friend!
> . . . .
> Make, oh Lord, it be considered
> that this be eternal justice!
>
> (I, 116)

There follows a series of comments by minor characters in which Atila's death is repeatedly described as miserable, together with the justness of his punishment, the most severe which the Golden Age drama had to offer.[45] The play ends with an epilogue in which *Tragedy* advises everyone to perceive doctrine with which to awaken in themselves "divine virtue" (I, 117).

IV   La Cruel Casandra

The meaning of the last sentence above and particularly the necessity to define virtue by the word "divine" is essential to the conclusions set forth in the final chapter of this book. The point is reinforced in the prologue to Virués' *Cruel Casandra:*

> . . . virtue is advisable in the youth,
> in the old it is honorable and delightful,
> useful to the poor; to the rich, rich adornment;
> glory to the happy, to the unhappy consolation,
> luster of the nobility, *and great nobility*
> *for those who by their blood don't have it,*
> and finally the greatest good there is on earth.

(I, 58; italics mine)[46]

In this play, which attempts to display "examples of virtue, although shown perhaps by its opposite, vice" (prologue, I, 58), the action is set in motion because the prince believes he has lost his honor through the infidelity of his wife. Through the machinations of Casandra, the prince is made to find his favorite, Filadelfo, in the princess' chambers and kills both Filadelfo and the princess, though at different times. Filadelfo is his first victim and he orders the body to be buried secretly, "together with my insult and my affront," killing the princess afterward so that "I may hand over my affront to oblivion" (I, 82).

It is important to note that the prince does not carry out these murders in order to assert his *hombría*. As Américo Castro points out, personages of the highest rank possessed immemorial honor and it was licit for them and dramatically possible to avenge themselves in secret."[47] Virués himself suggests his sympathy for the victim as Fabio soliloquizes:

> Ah, troubled and luckless princess!
> you have a chance for a great proof
> of your Christian breast and sanity;
> but, who can know what to do
> in such a bitter and fierce misfortune?
> Have patience, and only in death;
> in it you will be an innocent martyr.
>
> (I, 83)

Fabio's words are a reflection of Virués' own vacillation. The final couplet suggests a stoic resignation but Virués does not present the princess' death on the stage, nor does anyone relate her attitude toward her death. The only reaction is that of the murderer himself, who considers his wife's death a just punishment resulting in "eternal infamy and miserable death" (I, 87). We have heard similar words before, in reference to the death of Atila. At that time, however, the commentary was provided by minor characters at the end of the drama, much in the fashion of a classical chorus. This time, it is only the opinion of the self-righteous assassin. In short, Virués leaves in doubt the interpretation of the princess' death. As for the prince himself, he is killed in an unusual duel with Fabio, in which the prince simultaneously kills Fabio while Casandra, the witness, is also mortally wounded by a stray blow of one of the swords.

I find *Cruel Casandra* the least satisfying of all of Virués' dramas. Although the prologue may be taken at face value—regarding everything and everybody as examples of the lack of virtue and consequently adding evidence to the interpretation suggested with respect to Atila, namely, that Virués does not approve of the killing of an adulterous wife—there is little to be gleaned from this work. I must agree with Atkinson that every one of the deaths in this play is void of inner necessity and that "no amount of searching will find virtue succoured in the course of *La cruel Casandra.*"[48]

V   La Infelice Marcela

The clearest treatment of the concepts dealt with by Virués appears in *La infelice Marcela* (Unfortunate Marcela). Princess Marcela of England is on her way to rejoin her husband, Prince Landino of León, who had entrusted her safety to Count Alarico. The latter violates the trust placed in him and makes advances to Marcela. Because of his love, Alarico declares himself to be an enemy "of holy loyalty, of nobility and of everything honor carries with it" (I, 120). [49] Tersilo, another knight, warns him:

> Control yourself, I beg you, and don't try
> in one moment to lose what in a thousand years
> you couldn't gain, even if you go along
> always defeating countless wrongs.

(I, 121) [50]

A fight ensues and Tersilo is mortally wounded. His first reaction is to bemoan the injustice of his death after "defending innocent chastity with such zeal" (I, 122), but upon reflection he realizes that his noble defense of Marcela (a morally virtuous deed) has brought him that better and glorious form of life, the life of honor. This explains why he begs his blood not to cease flowing from the wound because "through honorable endeavors death is glorious life" (I, 123).

Although Menón (*Great Semíramis*) had welcomed death as "the great healer of people," not since Dido have we heard anyone refer to death as glorious, surely no surprise in view of the fact that Tersilo is the only character since Dido who performs a self-sacrificing deed. It is interesting to note that in both cases, the preservation of chastity (a specific kind of moral virtue) manifests the generic moral virtue of the character and provides the basis for the other and longer-lasting life of honor.

Curiously, Tersilo's death is never presented on stage nor is it ever explicitly stated, although it seems clear from his long monologue that he considers himself moribund. Sargent mentions "the unexplained dropping out of the action of Tersilo," [51] but Mérimée (p. 348) concludes that he dies. In view of Virués' penchant for deaths, I must reach the conclusion that some significance attaches to his reluctance to state definitely that Tersilo died. The answer is given by Tersilo himself:

> I expect life from fame
> so long as the world shall live.
> This divine secret
> is clear to me and patent
> since for the sake of giving me immense glory
> I have been given this light pain.

(I, 123)

Tersilo has triumphed over death by having attained fame, which in turn gives him life, that second variety which, as Jorge Manrique had explained, is not eternal either, but better and longer. Tersilo clearly understands the distinction between physical life and the life of fame ("I expect life from fame") on the one hand, and the difference between eternal life and the life of fame ("so long as the *world* shall live") on the other.

Tersilo's heroism is immediately contrasted by the cowardly reaction of the shepherd to whom Marcela turns for protection: "I don't know, madam, for here comes the man and I'm not waiting around here any longer; may God defend you" (I, 124). Thus Marcela is at the mercy of Alarico, whose vicious actions have already caused him to lose his honor (i.e., the moral sort), as is evidenced by the declarations of Tersilo, Marcela, and Alarico himself. The other sort of honor, whose ultimate source is the king and hence is dependent upon external recognition, is also present in the character of Alarico, deriving from the favors bestowed upon him by the prince, "who gave me the estate and title of count" (I, 132). But even this brand of honor is now taken away from him as he and Marcela are captured by a group of bandits, causing Alarico to lament, "Yesterday a great lord; today an aggrieved slave?" as he comprehends his own guilt:

> since I tried upon so many
> to inflict unbridled affrontery,
> on the princess, on Landino,
> on my honor, on the just heavens,
> for the sake of such an infamous desire
> to attempt such folly!
>
> (I, 131)

The capture of Alarico and Marcela places the latter at the mercy of the bandits. Felina, one of the women among the bandits, wishes to keep Marcela as a slave and take possession of her clothes and jewels, but Oronte, a lord of a nearby castle, temporarily rescues Marcela. Felina is furious and asks Formio, leader of the bandits and lover of Felina, to recover the princess. Fornio considers Oronte's rescue of Marcela as an insult to him and hurries after them.[52]

While Formio is chasing after Oronte, Felina falls in love with Alarico and plans to poison Formio. The latter learns of the relationship between Felina and Alarico and similarly plans to poison

Felina. Like Atila and the prince in *Cruel Casandra,* Formio is a man who, unfaithful himself, feels obligated to kill the woman who is unfaithful to him. Unfortunately, the poison which Felina and Formio prepare for each other is inadvertently consumed by the "unfortunate Marcela."

Scholars generally agree that the death of Marcela serves no purpose. She had, of course, expressed the desire for death on several occasions during her captivity as the only alternative to Formio's expressed intention to make her his wife (despite the fact that she was already married to Landino), but in view of the denouement, her rescue was imminent and hence the dramatic necessity for death disappeared. However, such a conclusion reveals the critics' continued insistence on interpreting this and other plays by Virués as classical tragedies. Since one cannot deny that *Unfortunate Marcela* is not a tragedy in the classical sense of that term, it follows that it is inconsistent to base interpretations of the play on classical precepts. Marcela's death does serve to illustrate the vanity of mundane glories, the fact that death may come at any time and that if one dies with honor death is not to be feared—concepts quite consistent with the concepts dealt with thus far in this book.

In the prologue, Virués presented the example of a shipwreck, commenting that "such is the hope of humans, so long as it is based on fragile things" (I, 118). Now, as Marcela consumes the poison, her memory brings back the earthly glory she once enjoyed:

> That I actually had a lady-in-waiting
> on this side and another on that side
> when in my drawing-room I wanted
> to drink while having a bite to eat?
> That the page, that the duenna,
> that the butler would come to respond
> to everything I longed for,
> just by my making a single sign?

But she is aware that "that which memory represents, passed like human glory" and consequently begs:

> Memory, stop it now,
> for my greatest trouble is this:
> let it not cost us our chastity,
> for we can stand everything.

> Everything, although death be
> eating and drinking like this,
> Marcela will suffer here
> provided her honor she here retains.

(I, 143)

At this point the poison takes effect and Marcela is overcome by a strange sleep, the most peaceful death in the dramas of Virués.[53] It is significant, then, that Marcela takes the poison unwittingly, death being quite unexpected ("And how strange and sudden!"). This gives added meaning to the previously cited prologue of *Cruel Casandra,* in which Virués declared that "virtue is advisable in the youth." Death, as we saw in Artieda's *The Lovers,* may overtake one by surprise and in the flower of one's youth, but if one has honor (moral virtue, here again symbolized by chastity) at the time of death, "we can stand everything."

When Prince Landino comes upon the dead body of Marcela, his first reaction is the desire for suicide. However he follows the advice of one of his knights: "Sir, that is not the way to achieve your life, but rather to have eternal death" (I, 144). This is, in short, the Christian attitude to suicide, quite contrary to the sweeping generalization made by Atkinson:

In the end it is taken as normal that anyone who has had the misfortune to stray into the tragedy must *ipso facto* expect a tragic end. Virués in short kills off everybody as the most satisfactory way of bringing down the curtain. Even so the romantic *comedia* will marry off everybody in the last act.[54]

VI   *The Anticipation of the Comedia*

It is essential not to lose sight of what Atkinson is really saying in spite of himself. Although he is, like so many others, insisting on calling it a tragedy and then criticizing it for failing to measure up to the inner and outer requirements of classical tragedy, he misses not only the significance of death in these works but actually fails to see the importance of his own comparison with what he terms "the romantic *comedia.*"[55] It is precisely this gradual approximation to (hence anticipation of) the Lopean *comedia* that enables us first to understand the works and then to see Virués' place in the development of the national *comedia*.

Sargent similarly skirts this important aspect by at once acknowledging and nearly ridiculing it:

Tragedy persists—catastrophes increase in proportion as Virués moves farther from his classic masters. . . . *Marcela* spares the hero, but he is with difficulty restrained from suicide! Yet tragedy does not hold undisputed sway; just as we have seen in *Casandra, Atila* and *Marcela* the romantic tale pushing out historical tradition, so elements of comedy crowd tragic elements in the two latter.[56]

Sargent relegates to a footnote the perceptive observation of Bouterwek, made a century ago, that "some of Virués' tragedies might almost be called *comedias*."[57] Even more surprising is Sargent's conclusion that "perhaps it was well that [Virués] did drop drama, for by the time he had written *Marcela*, though he had gained in technique, he was *approaching too closely current concepts* [italics mine] to make any startlingly original contributions to its development."[58]

Gwynne Edwards observes that Virués

remains in accord with the conventions of the *comedia* in his concern with moral issues and their illustration through specific themes. . . . In relation to the source material, Virués' significant contribution, therefore, was one of organizing and reshaping something loose and episodic in order to develop certain themes. In this respect he is a clear forerunner of the great Golden Age dramatists. . . . [59]

It is necessary to recall that Lope de Vega himself credited Virués with having established an integral part of the structure of the *comedia* (the three-act format) and an essential part of the stuff of the *comedia* (the blending of the tragic and the comic). Moreover, the introduction of the *romance* verse form to the drama has been shown to be Virués' innovation. With regard to the honor concept, the final chapter of this book will deal with its function and Virués' role in its development in greater detail. Suffice it to say at this point that the present chapter contains enough substantiation for the statement that the essence of the honor concept as developed by Lope and his followers is already present as a central theme in Virués. Sargent, despite her previously cited statements, concludes the main body of her book by writing that "the historian of human endeavor will recognize that the chasm from Cueva to Lope, incomprehensible if taken at a single leap, becomes a possibility when bridged by the [Valencian] erudites whose drama, faulty as it was, gloriously spanned the way to a *Siglo de Oro*."[60]

CHAPTER 4

Tárrega

A great deal of confusion exists concerning the biography of the Canon Francisco Agustín Tárrega. His birthplace is in doubt: Mesonero Romanos,[1] Barrera,[2] and Martí Grajales[3] all maintain that he was born in the city of Valencia, but Juliá states that it was in the diocese of Segorbe, perhaps in that very town (p. lxxiii), thus agreeing with Mérimée (p. 457), who thought the poet's place of birth to be outside Valencia, in Segorbe or some other village of the diocese of Segorbe. More recently, Ebersole simply states that Tárrega was a native of Valencia.[4]

Similar confusion exists concerning the year of Tárrega's birth. Schaeffer thinks it was soon after 1550,[5] Mérimée suggests at the earliest in 1553, probably a little later, around 1555 or 1556, Juliá thinks it was between 1553 and 1555, thus agreeing with Serrano Cañete,[6] whereas Martí Grajales believes it to have been between 1554 and 1556.[7]

Whether or not he was a native of the city itself, Juliá considers him a Valencian, because he lived among Valencians constantly and the trips he took lacked any importance for his cultural development. "Two times he went to Madrid," writes Juliá, "and with such swiftness that it can be shown that his life was based in Valencia" (*loc. cit.*). On the other hand, Crawford's fundamental book, repeatedly cited in the present study, namely, *Spanish Drama Before Lope de Vega*, does not even mention Tárrega, from which Froldi (pp. 117–18) concludes that Crawford evidently considered Tárrega to be a simple disciple of Lope. However, as Valbuena Prat points out, "one can see by the very chronology that he was more a *pre-lopista* of the previous generation than a disciple of the creator of *Peribáñez*, and many of these aspects can be noted in his heroic *comedias* and those with a contemporary theme."[8]

Tárrega was a charter member of the *Academia de los Nocturnos* under the pseudonym of *Miedo* ("Fear"). It was he who designated the themes for the readings and had the right to admit or reject applicants who wished to be members of the academy.[9]

In July, 1600, there took place in Valencia a series of festivals in honor of the arrival of the remains of Saint Vicente Ferrer. It fell to Tárrega to judge the poetry of the festivities, as he had done on many occasions. Of the 123 compositions that were submitted, eighteen were awarded prizes, among them poems by the following Valencians: ". . . Gaspar Aguilar and Doctor Virués won the topaze and the diamond, respectively, for their sonnets; D. Gaspar Mercader, the silver mirror and a pouch of amber for his quatrains; . . . and Carlos Boil, the silver vase and the green sash for his octaves. . . . "[10]

The Valencian dramatist Miguel Beneyto summed up the high esteem in which Tárrega was held by his contemporaries in some verses dedicated to the founders of the Academy:

> [President Catalán] has the famous Tárrega
>   at his side,
> for whose sake the world has need of fames,
> since just one is not enough to honor him.
> His rare genius, his profound knowledge,
> his serious, heroic, and miraculous verse;
> the foremost in the world and without peer[11]

In our own century, Martí Grajales laments that Tárrega is so little known despite his undeniable and capital importance, pointing out that, although he did not reach the height of Guillén de Castro, he is, nonetheless, superior to all the rest of the dramatists of the Valencian school and even to many imitators of Lope who became known later in the theaters of Madrid.[12] After quoting a passage from Lope de Vega's *La Dorotea*, which was written in Lope's youth and in which Lope mentions the great poets of that age, among whom he includes Tárrega, Juliá exclaims, "How the impression which Canon Tárrega made upon Lope from the first moments of his arrival in Valencia is revealed!"[13] Froldi (p. 125) goes even further, asserting unequivocally that "Tárrega truly initiates what we call the Spanish *comedia*."[14] Unfortunately, Froldi does not consider it his purpose to analyze Tárrega's dramas from within and we are left with the tempting suggestion that such a study would "give new and useful indications to qualify an author unjustly sacrificed by the

critics." Froldi concludes by saying that for now he has shown that
Tárrega's works "present the fundamental characteristics of the
Spanish *comedia*" (p. 128).

An observation by Gillet—which compares death in the late
fifteenth-century masterpiece by Fernando de Rojas, *La Celestina*,
and the early sixteenth-century *Himenea* by Torres Naharro—can
be applied to the difference in the treatment of the same subject by
Virués and Tárrega. Gillet notes that "the suicide of Melibea has
been replaced by an ending suited to . . . Torres Naharro's
prophetic concept of the *comedia* of Lope de Vega . . . : not death,
but only its passing shadow."[15]

This contrast, which Green considers a consequence of the difference between the tragic and the comic,[16] is evident when we
compare the theater of Virués with that of Tárrega. This is not to say
that death does not occur in Tárrega's plays—nor, of course, did
Gillet mean to imply that death is absent from Lope's plays—but
rather that in the *comedia* death is not the inevitable ending. The
reason for this is that, whereas tragedy (including the form of
tragedy peculiar to Artieda and Virués) had to present the characters' end, comedy (including the often unfunny form of *comedia*
peculiar to the Spanish Golden Age) is not necessarily concerned
with endings at all, being content to portray episodes, affairs, or
adventures in the lives of the characters.

I El Prado de Valencia

Not death then, but only its passing shadow, is precisely what we
find in what may be Tárrega's first play,[17] *El Prado de Valencia* (The
Meadow of Valencia), in which the heroine, Laura, finds herself the
victim of a series of lies on the part of several of the other characters
in the play who make it appear that Laura is in love with Count
Fabricio. Her fiancé, Don Juan, prepares to abandon her because
he has been led to believe the calumnies against Laura, considering
as incontrovertible evidence the fact that Laura had accepted a
letter from the count, a compromising position for a woman.[18] Juan
therefore considers himself relieved of his promise to marry her,
"since the pen which writes the letter erases my obligations" (I,
181).

Thereupon occurs the first encounter with the shadow of death:
although Laura has remained faithful to Juan, his departure would
be a sign to others of her infidelity. She begs him to let her accompany him, for he now represents her reputation:

> Let me follow my honor,
> for I can't live without it.
> For you're taking my reputation away from me
> and leaving me your offense.
>
> (I, 181)

Since his departure would be equivalent to his taking away her reputation (hence honor), Laura wishes she could die, because "no one can hide the errors of a woman better than the grave" (I, 182). But this momentary desire for death is quickly dispelled by the appearance of Teodoro, uncle of both Laura and Juan, who wants them to marry as soon as possible, for people have begun to gossip about the delay, which Teodoro fears will lead to dishonor, "for great delay converts excuse into discredit," and, although both Juan and Laura share the same relationship to the uncle, Teodoro takes Laura's side because she is "the party where the damage lies," urging a prompt wedding, "for this is the best way" (I, 182). So it is indicated that death for Laura is unnecessary, for her reputation (honor) can be preserved through marriage.

However, the lies and calumnies continue to such an extent that Laura seems unable to extricate herself from the dilemma. She blames it all on her original error: the acceptance of the letter from the count: "How much discredit is bound to follow the woman who accepts a piece of paper!" (I, 187).

Laura is quick to learn from her experience, however. Aware that her troubles are the result of her innocence and ignorance of the exigencies of society (the acceptance of the letter) on the one hand, and the deception of society (her maligning acquaintances) on the other, Laura overcomes the former by acknowledging it and thus triumphing over it:

> I took the letter then blamelessly
> and now I wouldn't excuse myself,
> for I know that even as a formality
> it is not good to receive letters.
>
> (I, 216)

With regard to the deception of society, Laura overcomes that by acknowledging *it* with a deception of her own. Having arranged matters so that Juan agrees to hide and witness the events, Laura has herself and her lying companions captured by a band of Moors (in reality Christians hired by Laura for the occasion) who pretend to prepare to kill them all. At this point, one by one, the calumniators beg for confession prior to death. While Juan listens unseen, they all confess their defamatory actions and tales about Laura's behavior. As one of them declares guilt ("I mounted the fabrication which has brought me to my death"), Juan realizes the truth: "Pardon is worth the whole world" (I, 227).

The shadow of death has restored Laura's reputation but not before she had learned to cope with the nature of society. Although her initial reaction to the loss of her reputation was the desire for death, she heeded the advice that through marriage she could restore that reputation. But, since her marriage in turn depended upon that same reputation to provide the necessary honor (the Spanish *honra*) for her to marry honorably, Laura had first to restore her reputation by learning to cope with the deceitful nature of the society which had deprived her of that *honra*. Through the deception which she herself devised, Laura restored her reputation and hence her honor, enabling her to marry Juan and thus have that honor publicly recognized. We have here, then, a typical *comedia de capa y espada*, in which transgression is of a comic nature, thus permitting one of the characters to remark at the conclusion that "death ends up in pleasure" (I, 228).[19] As Froldi points out (p. 125), the motifs are many which make of this work a true *comedia*.[20]

II   Las Suertes Trocadas y Torneo Venturoso

In similar fashion does the shadow of death cloud the lives of the characters in *Las suertes trocadas y torneo venturoso* (Reversed Fortunes and Fortunate Tourney). The marquis is in love with the duke's daughter, Maurelia, who is in love with the count, as is her sister, whom the count loves. The marquis asks the duke's majordomo, Fulgencio, how to remove the obstacle which lies between him and Maurelia. Fulgencio advises him that the count should be killed and offers to do it for him, considering himself justified in such an action because the duke had promised Maurelia to the marquis. Accordingly, when he sees the count talking to Maurelia, Fulgencio attacks him with a dagger, rationalizing his attempted murder by explaining that he represents the duke: "for although he is count Hiracio, I am the duke in the palace since I look out for his honor" (I, 394).

Despite the insult to his person—"holding me in so little esteem" (I, 395)—the count believes Fulgencio's lie that the dagger was intended for another and forgives the majordomo. Sabina, who had witnessed the attempted assassination and had, in fact, been the one who saved the count's life by staying Fulgencio's hand, does not approve, stating in an aside that the count "already considers life abhorrent, since he is not attending to the injury" (*ibid.*).

The count's punishment for dismissing the affront to his person is to lose first his lady and then his identity in madness, for he has lost his *raison d'être:* "He who suffers such injuries, for what purpose should he live?" (I, 421). He therefore seeks to deny his existence through death—"Everything bores and annoys me, in search of death I go" (I, 422)—because, "Grievances make me fall, disdains drive me crazy, and seeing myself held in little esteem is ending my life quickly" (I, 423). Instead of physical death, however, the count prefers merely to deny his identity and forces an impoverished student to change clothes with him. The student is overjoyed ("for I am another than the one I was") and the count has denied his own existence: "for I am death's shadow and I cease being the count" (I, 423).

The count's madness is symbolic not merely of a personal, individual loss of honor. It is, in addition, symbolic of the demands of society, as explained by the marquis:

> He who doesn't esteem his honor at all,
> him I judge to be completely crazy,
> for to hold oneself in little esteem these days,
> God knows what damage it causes.
> Such a person neither respects others
> nor attends to or thinks of anything,
> for once shame is lost
> there is no ugliness he wouldn't take on.
> . . . .
> for he is like a woman without it
> and he undertakes any treachery at all.
>
> (I, 432)

We have here in Tárrega an interesting conception of honor, not limited to the egoistic and individualized notion of exaggerated pride in one's reputation but extending to the need for one's actions to be honorable because of the effect of those actions upon others, that is, society.[21] Thus a man who loses his self-esteem and consequently his honor is likely to have little regard for the rest of

society and there is no telling how far he will go in his shameless-
ness. Accordingly, the duke wishes the count punished as an example to society, "so that others will be frightened," which is echoed
by the aged Horacio: "Punishment for tyrants serves as a mirror to
everybody else" (I, 432).

That the count's predicament is but a temporary one is revealed
by the twofold nature of its cause. Since his loss of honor is the result
of his refusal to avenge the disrespect shown him, and his loss of
love is a consequence of the disdain shown him by Sabina because of
a mixup of a love letter, the comical nature of the loss of love belies
the gravity of the loss of honor. Thus the problem is resolved in a
tourney in which the count, still disguised, defeats his opponent
(Sabina in disguise) and wins Sabina's hand. In short, he has regained his honor by winning the match and at the same time has
regained Sabina's love. The comic treatment of the count's problem
is similar to that of Laura's in *The Meadow of Valencia*. As Laura had
done, so the count has had to learn to cope with the deceptive
nature of life and society. The shadow of death into which the count
transforms himself ("I am death's shadow") teaches him that the
negation of one's self is not the solution to the problems of life, for,
while dressed as the student, the count comes upon Sabina, who
confesses her love for him but refuses to let him touch her because
she will not believe that he *is* the count. Not until he restores his
rank by taking part in the tourney, that is, by facing life, does he
regain her love (and his existence and honor) as he reenters society
which now accepts him once again: "for he ought to be fully es-
teemed" (I, 441).

In similar fashion does the marquis learn that death does not solve
the problems of life. Because Maurelia prefers the count, the
marquis despairs and wishes to commit suicide—"Death will provide the remedy"—but Sabina convinces him of the madness of such
thinking and advises him to suffer with patience, for "after one time
comes another" (I, 399). She promises to help him enter Maurelia's
room. "I'm waking now from the dream," replies the marquis, now
ready to face life: "To you I owe honor and life, for you made a tool
of life" (I, 400). In other words, by facing life one may retain both
life and honor. After Sabina leaves, the marquis soliloquizes:

> For everything there is a remedy in this life,
> death by itself undoes everything,

there is no evil that does not pass with time,
and within hours a good breast gets rid of it.

But where can there be a woman so daring
that she does not burn up in amorous flames,
and not get caught in Cupid's net
already submitting to the desires of another?

For an unhappy and unfortunate one to die,
ends honor and glory once and for all,
like the swan whose final end is a sweet song.

I shall give that count a fameless grave,
enjoying my victory with my own hands
for to honor oneself at the expense of a
traitor is not terrible.

(I, 400)

It appears that the marquis still has much to learn. Although he has rejected suicide as the solution to his problems, he still entertains murder as a way out. The first quatrain of the sonnet shows that he has heard Sabina's advice about the healing effect of time but has failed to grasp its full significance. Recognizing that there is a remedy to every problem in life (i.e., that there is no need to flee from life) and that death may achieve this for him—not his own death any longer but that of his rival—the youthful and impatient marquis prefers to act now rather than wait for the passage of time to have its effect. The first tercet of the sonnet manifests his belief that the death of an unhappy, unfortunate person does not restore fortune or happiness but, on the contrary, puts an end to honor and glory, being merely one's swan song, a sweet but nonetheless final end to the good as well as the bad.[22]

While the first quatrain and the first tercet reveal the marquis' reasoning, the second quatrain and tercet reveal his plan: to seduce Maurelia by pretending to be someone else to whom she would readily yield, since, once her passion is aroused, no woman can escape Cupid's net; second, to kill the count, considering himself justified because he, the marquis, had been promised Maurelia by the duke, thus making the count a traitor in the marquis' eyes.

Consequently, while the marquis is willing to face life, he is not yet ready to face it as himself. In short, as the count had done, the marquis denies his own identity by believing that he will succeed only by being someone else. Ironically, the marquis is caught at the window by Fulgencio, who mistakes him for the count and attempts to kill him but is himself wounded by the marquis. At last, the marquis has become aware of his error, for in the wounding of his friend he sees his own dishonor, occasioned by his refusal to be himself:

> Was I crazy or foolish?
> What deeds did I attempt
> in ceasing to be who I was
> if I don't watch out for my friend?
> What resulted from the deed?
> . . . .
>
> Against my honor I fired the shot,
> and I'm provoking myself to rage,
> holding my blood in little esteem,
> since I'm not looking out for yours.

(I, 418)

Once again the marquis expresses a desire for death, but this time not for selfish reasons. He wishes he could die in his friend's stead:

> Let me bleed myself drop by drop,
> for the sake of my giving you new life.
> But if you like at this moment,
> like the noble Pelican,
> there will come forth for you, and still I gain,
> the sustenance from my veins.

(I, 419)

No longer does he use the simile of the swan, whose final song is followed by the end of glory. Now he prefers to emulate the pelican who, legend has it, feeds her young with her own blood. This self-sacrificing desire of the marquis restores life to his wounded friend as the shadow of death passes: "With your love and friendship, you give life to my heart," says Fulgencio, "your will raises me, alive after being dead and defunct" (I, 419).

His lessons learned, the marquis is now at last ready to face life and, like the count, wins the hand of his beloved in a tourney, subsequently admitting that it was he who had entered Maurelia's room, "for it was I alone who that was" (I, 441).

Wardropper's thesis, cited earlier, that the humoristic *comedia* be viewed as a preparation for the more serious facets of life after marriage, is well supported in *Reversed Fortunes*, for in the background of the comical treatment of the problems that beset the count and the marquis, stands the very serious figure of the old duke.[23] His long soliloquy, with its emphasis on the inexorability of death, is reminiscent of Artieda:

> . . . for our lives end
> just when man forgets dying most.
> . . . .
> To put certainty in this earth
> where there is no firmness in anything,
> is to live with deception and suspicion.
> . . . .
> for we only take with us from this life
> the good which we try to do in it.

The duke goes on to list a number of real and fictitious heroic figures of the past, such as Caesar, Alexander, and Achilles, and asks:

> Did people like that escape death?
> . . . .
> No, for sure; but their name remained,
> the fame of their deeds and their renown.
> . . . .
> The only thing that stays always and remains
> is good behavior and habits of people;
> also honor, which never perishes.
> . . . .
> for the rest is earth, dust, and nothing,
> and the soul, above all else, raised.

> (I, 388–89)

We have here, of course, a series of familiar concepts: the inexorability of death, the fact that death arrives when least expected, the deceptive nature of earthly life, the *ubi sunt* theme, and the ephemeral character of mundane things. We also find here in Tárrega a continuation of a theme noted in Artieda and Virués (and of course earlier in Jorge Manrique), namely, that honor survives death. However, what is significant here is that the duke puts emphasis on the good that one tries to do in this life, on the behavior of people, adding *almost* as an afterthought that "also" honor is imperishable.[24] Tárrega would seem to be emphasizing the social consequences of human behavior, an observation given further

support by the previously cited speech on the effect upon society of
honorable and dishonorable men, as well as the inclusion of another
highly important sentence in the duke's soliloquy—"Prudent is he
who accepts good advice and amends what he erred through his
weakness"—all of which would suggest that Tárrega's message is
that man in his moments of weakness commits many errors but he
who is prudent will profit from the errors and mend his ways. This is
indeed one of the subthemes of this play; that it forms an integral
part in the development of the major honor theme of the *comedia*
will be elaborated in the final chapter of this book.

III   El Esposo Fingido

In *El esposo fingido* (The False Husband), Tárrega once again
presents an unmarried woman, Teodosia, who must learn to cope
with the deceitful nature of life and to preserve her honor. I refer to
her as an unmarried woman, for, although she at first believes herself to be married, she later learns that the man in question, Arnaldo, is already married.[25] Teodosia's "marriage" had been arranged
by her avaricious father,[26] but the marriage has never been
consummated (I, 261). However, as Teodosia herself describes it,
she had responded "with cowardly obedience" to her greedy father's
wishes. This, then, has been Teodosia's flaw: the surrender, through
"cowardly obedience," to her father's plans instead of following her
own amorous inclinations toward the impoverished Honorio who, as
his name implies, is "poor out of sheer honorability" (I, 237).

Accordingly, it is Teodosia's honor that is tarnished by the bigamy
as she realizes that she would have retained her honor had she
remained faithful to Honorio:

> Now, poverty, I know
> how sane and safe I was
> in my reasoning for esteeming
> a poverty which I loved
> which, being lowly, I forgot.
>
> (I, 238)

Like the marquis in *Reversed Fortunes*, Teodosia believes that
murder is a way out and consequently poisons her "husband's" other
wife, Clodosinda: "I avenged with her death my blood as a woman"
(I, 257). As punishment for this act of murder, Teodosia is buried
alive together with the apparently dead Clodosinda. However, the

potion has only made it appear that Clodosinda is dead. Teodosia interprets this as the intervention of God (I, 261), and the two women forgive each other, whereupon Honorio appears and frees them from their tomb, giving them new life: "You take me out of death's hands . . . for, since you save me, well can I say that you resuscitate me," exclaims Clodosinda, while Teodosia promises lifelong love to Honorio: "I want to leave death to serve you with my life" (I, 261–62).

Before they leave, however, the two women appear before Arnaldo in the tomb. Male relatives of both women decide that Arnaldo must be the one to die and remain in the tomb. However, Honorio saves Arnaldo as well, at which point the two women forgive Arnaldo. The shadow of death has taught them all the value of forgiveness, as well as the lesson that honor and love are achieved not by money and force but by virtue and will. Although Mérimée was annoyed by Tárrega's frequent use of suddenly happy endings after a series of catastrophes, it should be noted that in the *comedias* studied thus far, the comic nature of the unmarried people's situations has prevented true catastrophes as only the shadow of death brings about the turn of events which leads the characters on the road to moral rectitude.

IV   La Duquesa Constante

The use of a potion to give the semblance of death and a person buried alive are elements of yet another play by Tárrega, *La duquesa constante* (The Constant Duchess). In this work, the duke, happily married to Flaminia, is called to Spain and asks Governor Torcato to watch over Flaminia during his absence. Unknown to the duke, however, is Torcato's desire to seduce Flaminia. Consequently he does not grasp the literal meaning behind Torcato's assurance that Flaminia will have "her soul wherever you may go and her body here in my power" (I, 494).

During the duke's absence, then, Torcato makes repeated advances to Flaminia, having sent his own wife out of town. But the married Flaminia is not the unmarried Laura of *The Meadow of Valencia* and refuses to accept letters and jewels sent to her by Torcato, for this is not a laughable comedy but a serious play dealing with "the problems of married people, sacramentally made one flesh by divine grace; any interference with this divinely ordained state is a kind of blasphemy, followed inevitably by retribution and mis-

fortune."[27] That Flaminia is fully aware of this is shown by the
answer she gives Torcato when he asks why she stubbornly resists
him: "I am the wife of the man who loves all the way from Spain [the
play takes place in Italy], leaving aside *the most important thing*,
which is God and my obligation" (I, 509; italics mine).

Torcato, on the other hand, does not understand. Not only does
he propose to kill his own wife in order to marry Flaminia, but upon
learning that Flaminia would prefer to die rather than be unfaithful
to her husband, he attempts to explain to her that the desire for
death is contrary to the will of God, "because Heaven is all peace
and a disdain is odious war" (I, 513). Torcato's confusion of the peace
of Heaven—which is in reality reflected in the sacramental union of
matrimony—with his own petty obsession to achieve a lustful
conquest without resistance ("odious war"), reveals his ignorance of
the true nature of marriage and virtue. Flaminia's desire for death is
not based on despair. Torcato had given her an hour's time in which
to think matters over. Consequently, when she returns, her conclusion is based not upon a sudden whim but upon deliberation:

> Life is an uncertain journey,
> death more general,
> and perhaps with some other trouble
> awaits me at that door.
>
> . . . .
> I die cheerfully and blameless;
> I carry my breast secure,
> and since I am not seeking [death],
> I present force as my excuse.
>
> (I, 512–13)

Although she recognizes the ephemeral nature of man's stay on
earth, Flaminia does not actively seek death for escapist motives, for
she is aware of the greater uncertainty that awaits her in death.
Considering herself free from blemish, she does not regard her
decision to accept death as suicide, inasmuch as it is a forced death
because, of the two alternatives available to her—acquiescence to
Torcato's demands or death—the former would involve her volun-
tary transgression of the marriage sacrament, whereas the latter
solution is death at the hands of another, that is, martyrdom. Accordingly, when she drinks the potion, she feels not only at ease but
stronger:

It already seems that I feel
soothed, friend, and stronger,
since I've felt death
residing in my breast.

(I, 513)

When the duke returns, he overhears a conversation between a page and a captain in which Flaminia's death is described as follows:

PAGE: Like a wilted flower which early
        surrenders to hurried and stern fate,
        her gentle body paid the human debt.
        and her pure soul through the pure air
        rose to enjoy the immortal beauty,
        leaving us here doubt and sadness.

CAPTAIN: Doubt? and of what?

PAGE: Of seeing how sudden
        and without external cause her death was,
        for not even Dr. Cardano can guess it;
        but what is being murmured and imagined,
        I'll tell you in your ear.

(I, 519)

The inexorability of death is once again expressed here by the page, but the beautiful image of the flower and the purity of the soul receive discordant support from the final line of the page's first speech: there is doubt among the people. The answer to the captain's question brings to mind Heredia's comment about the death of Marcilla in Artieda's *The Lovers* ("who killed him?"). At that time I observed that the normal reaction on learning of the death of a youth is to conclude that someone killed him and that Heredia's question served to emphasize the absence of that someone, causing us to concentrate on Marcilla himself. Tárrega is not quite as subtle as Artieda and makes it obvious that people are drawing their own conclusions. What those conclusions are, Tárrega does leave to our imagination, for we do not hear what the page whispers in the captain's ear. Nor does the duke, but he has heard enough and suspects the worst: that Flaminia was unfaithful to him, thus leaving him without honor.

That the duke's possible loss of honor is more important to him than the loss of Flaminia is made clear when he confronts Torcato, who admits having killed Flaminia but claims he was only following the orders of the duke himself. (The duke had, in fact, left such orders in the event of his own death, false news of which had indeed reached Torcato.) The possible truth of Torcato's claim momentarily relieves the duke inasmuch as it would mean that Flaminia had remained faithful after all, thus leaving the duke with honor. Consequently, although the duke would like to kill Torcato, he also finds himself compelled to help Torcato prove his story:

> I must try to defend you,
> not to avoid your death,
> but because of my honor,
> considering as a favor
> what is the rigor of my luck;
> for that's what it will be if I understand
> that, free of all guilt,
> my wife, by dying, paid
> the punishment which excuses you;
> but, since she won by losing,
> let pleasure and life be lost
> provided that I haven't lost
> my fame, which is the best of all.
>
> (I, 524)

In other words, fame (by which he means his good name and reputation, the basis of honor) is not only more important than life but survives death, since it is possible for the duke to lose his life and nevertheless retain his fame. It is interesting to note that this is the duke's only consideration, whereas Flaminia had taken into account both "God and my obligation," a reflection of the dual nature of the state of matrimony, that is, divine as well as human.

The rumors that have been circulating about Flaminia affect not only the duke's fame or reputation but that of his aged and infirm uncle as well. As the latter tells his nephew, he has been concerned by the murmurings of the people, for they affect "our fame" (I, 526). Together the two men agree that Flaminia's body must be taken to the public square and be beheaded there where there is no deception so that she will lose "her fame publicly" (I, 528). Evidently, then, death alone is not a punishment unless it is accompanied by the loss of fame. Of course, this means the loss of *good* fame, for as Tirsia says, "Don't you know, Ganimedes, that fame never dies?" (I, 527).[28]

Having lost his own good fame and hence his honor, the duke seeks death, "for it is impossible to have life without honor" (I, 526). Wishing to commit suicide, the duke casuistically decides that the honor code outweighs the Christian attitude toward suicide:

> with just reason I agree
> to kill myself with my own hand;
> but no, for I am a Christian;
> but yes, for I am noble and sane.
>
> (I, 528)

The duke does not commit suicide, however, for his hand is stayed by the hand of Octavio reaching up from his own tomb. Octavio was the one who had prepared the poison for Flaminia, but, since it was only a potion which gave the temporary semblance of death, neither Flaminia nor Octavio (who was similarly "poisoned" by Torcato when he was informed that the duke was alive) has really died. The duke is now informed of his wife's heroic fidelity and returns to the public square to find Flaminia alive. Once more the shadow of death has permitted honor to be reaffirmed. Torcato, however, must die:

> I wish, in a town crier's voice,
> while this other fellow [Torcato] first loses,
> because of his great treachery, his life,
> to cause her lost fame
> to be restored completely.
>
> (I, 531)

Consequently, Torcato's death results in the loss of his own fame but restores Flaminia's fame (whose moral virtue is no longer in doubt) and the duke's honor. It is important to note, however, that it is not death *per se* that restores fame or honor, but the public nature ("in a town crier's voice") of the death that accomplishes this restoration.

V La Enemiga Favorable

It may not always be easy to restore honor, however, once the fame or reputation on which it is based has been placed in doubt. As we learn in *La enemiga favorable* (The Inimical Benefactress), "mended honor is never of the same cloth" (I, 611), even if the loss

of fame is the result of a lie, "because a lie and a stone tossed off
return in vain to the mouth and the hand" (I, 614). However, a more
favorable outcome is likely if honor is restored by the same person
who had originally cast aspersions on it: "honor must be returned to
you by the one who has doubted your honor" (I, 589).

In this play the married couple is a royal one: no less than the king
and queen. The former had been carrying on an affair with Laura,
sister of Count Polidoro. When the two women confront each other,
the queen calls Laura a liar and slaps her: Laura has been dishonored.

This scene provides some insight into Tárrega's conception of the
relationship of honor and the king. Northup, basing his conclusions
principally on the dramas of Calderón, points out that the king
cannot insult one of his subjects and "a blow administered by king to
subject need not, and could not be resented."[29] La Du, confining
his remarks to Valencia's Guillén de Castro, amplifies this observation: "It was taken for granted that an insult by the king, *or one of
royal blood,* did not offend" (italics mine).[30] For Tárrega, this
privilege apparently does not extend to the queen, for no one
doubts that Laura has been dishonored.

La Du further points out that in matters pertaining to the conduct
of the queen, the king was bound by the honor code in the same
fashion as was any husband of lower station.[31] In the Tárrega play
under discussion, there arises an interesting conflict of interests, for
not only is the king the husband of the woman who has caused the
dishonor, but Belisardo, brother of the queen and the betrothed of
Laura, also feels it his own duty to avenge the dishonor by killing
the queen. There occurs the following discussion:

> BELISARDO: Whom are you killing?
> KING: The queen. And whom are you killing?
> BELISARDO: My sister.
> . . . .
> KING: I, who have power around her, am bound to
> kill her for my honor.
> BELISARDO: I, too, for my wife.
> KING: She has offended my palace.
> BELISARDO: I'm bound this time to avenge my honor,
> which is lost.
> KING: Don't you see that I'm a judge?
> BELISARDO: Don't you see that I'm a husband?
> . . . .

> KING: Don't you avenge my justice.
> BELISARDO: And don't you avenge my wife.
> . . . .
> KING: No one is going to protect me.
> BELISARDO: No one is going to avenge me.
>
> (I, 593)

In other words, it is the king's duty to kill the queen because (1) she is his wife and has dishonored him by affronting another; (2) he is the king and it is an affront to him for anyone to commit an affront in the royal palace; (3) he is the king and consequently the supreme judge (i.e., no one else can decide a question which affects him). On the other hand, Belisardo feels it is *his* duty to kill the queen because (1) she is his sister and has dishonored him by affronting another, and (2) the recipient of the affront is his betrothed.

Tárrega himself avoids the resolution of this problem, for the scene is interrupted by the arrival of some courtiers. Technically, however, Belisardo is in the wrong, not only because he is not yet married to Laura and hence not yet responsible for her—Laura is the responsibility of her brother Polidoro, because "in the absence or after the death of the father it is the brother who emerges as defender of the family honor"[32]—but because on the other hand, *his* sister *is* married and consequently no longer his responsibility. His insistence upon taking precedence over the king in avenging the affront would imply that the king is shirking his responsibility, for only "in the case where the husband neglects to fulfill his duty to protect his honor and that of his wife does the charge revert to the brother."[33]

Belisardo, however, wants to marry Laura, and, although she has been promised to him by her brother, Laura herself does not care for Belisardo. Nevertheless, Laura and Belisardo join forces in a plan to discredit and kill the queen: Belisardo in the hope that this will assure him Laura's hand in marriage (since he would be the redeemer of her honor), and Laura in the hope that the queen's death would enable her to marry the king. To assure Belisardo's cooperation, Laura falsely promises to marry him: "Make me honorable, Belisardo, so that I can be yours afterward" (I, 594).

Death alone does not restore honor, as we have seen on other occasions, and, therefore, Belisardo plans not only to kill the queen but to deprive her of her honor: "Without honor, which is her glory, she must die" (I, 595).

Not content with this, however, Laura embarks upon a plan of her own. Dressing in mourning, she appears before the king and declares that she is without honor but that she herself cannot restore that honor: "Laura no longer avenges herself; she is lacking blood in her eye" (I, 597).[34] She promises the king that if he kills the queen, she will marry him, but if he refuses, then she will have to inform her brother of the affront. The king agrees and promises that "I shall give you my hand as I give him burial" (I, 598).

Belisardo also appears before the king, but, as noted, his plan is to discredit the queen. The gravity of dishonor is revealed by the conversation that takes place between the king and Belisardo after the latter has informed the king that what he has to say will kill him (i.e., kill the king):

> KING: Has the pope ordered me arrested?
> BELISARDO: More.
> KING: Did my troops turn back?
> BELISARDO: More.
> KING: Did my wife die?
> BELISARDO: More.
> KING: Did I lose my fleet?
> BELISARDO: More.
> . . . .
> KING: Well if it's more, doubtless I've been affronted.
>
> (I, 599)

The affront at which Belisardo hints is untrue but nonetheless affects the honor of the king. Told that the queen has been carrying on an affair with Duke Norandino, the king finds it hard to believe; yet,

> it is just reasoning for her to die,
> for a good king must not have
> a wife with a bad reputation.
> Through the satisfied masses
> the gossip goes from tongue to tongue,
> and *for an honorable breast,*
> *just that it could have been said*
> *is equivalent to its having been done.*
>
> (I, 611; italics mine)

Thus honor is not only based on reputation but may be equivalent to it, since for an honorable person what people say is as valid as what one has actually done. Despite the king's recognition of the folly of such reasoning—"How far opinion is from truth in the world!" (I,

597)—he is helpless to defy it: "I must follow [public] opinion" (I, 612). But this king is no Atila. His conscience plagues him:

> LAURA: Does it pain you to condemn her?
>
> . . . .
> If your passion condemns her,
> why do you kill her?
> KING: Because she's bad.
> LAURA: Why do you praise her?
> KING: Because she's good.
> . . . .
> LAURA: Don't you see that's contradicting yourself?
> . . . .
> Why is she bad?
> KING: Because it's being said.
> LAURA: And good?
> KING: Because she is.

(I, 612)

The seriousness of the situation and his love for the queen cause the king to forget his former infatuation with Laura. We saw earlier that the king is the supreme judge in such matters. We have also seen, however, that this king is plagued by his conscience, for he is aware that, despite the gossip and accusations of others (involving reputation and the outer form of honor), the queen is innocent (involving moral virtue and the inner form of honor). In other words, the king is caught in the dilemma alluded to earlier in this book, namely the conflicting tenets of the honor code and of Christianity.

Otis Green reminds us of the king in the *Cárcel de amor* (Prison of Love), who expressed the belief that vengeance is as important in matters of honor as Christian forgiveness is in other matters: "Such separation of a man's social conduct into two compartments by virtue of an ethical 'double truth' might be—indeed was—allowed a king in his public acts. In the individual conscience the problem could not be so simple. . . ."[35]

Accordingly, the king in Tárrega's play, mindful of the "condemned innocence, abhorred saintliness" of the queen, decides to leave matters to the truly Supreme Judge:

> let Irene get out of this entanglement,
> let the world know of this evil.
> I'm leaving, for I am afraid of God
> and I fear His eternity.

(I, 617)

In accordance with the beliefs inherited from the Goths, the queen's innocence or guilt and subsequent fate will be determined by combat, thus leaving the decision to God: "these are rules of the Gothic people" (I, 618).

Once again, however, it is only the shadow of death and not actual death that restores lost honor. Convinced that it must be the king himself who, as the husband whose honor is at stake, is taking the part of the challenger, the queen, who has never ceased loving him, chooses as her defender the weakest of the three who offer to defend her. What she does not know is that the king is one of the three defenders and that it is her brother Belisardo who is the challenger. The one she chooses as her defender turns out to be Laura, who, at the last moment, reveals her identity to Belisardo and persuades him to confess the truth.

It is not until this point, as the *comedia* reaches its happy ending, that Tárrega makes clear why the argument dealing with who was offended and whose duty it was to avenge the affront was never brought to a conclusion: the slap by the queen did not, after all, affront Laura, not because of the queen's royal status but because of her status as a woman:

> and aside from the fact that a woman
> does not affront anyone in anything,
> there can be no dishonor
> where there can be no sword.
>
> (I, 621)[36]

Are we to agree with one of the minor characters in this play as he comments that "perhaps all of this which just happened is madness" (I, 621) and conclude that the whole affair is to be interpreted as a farce? No, for as I pointed out earlier, at the time that the queen administered the slap, no one doubted that Laura had been dishonored. The fact that everyone in the play turned out to be incorrect does not alter the fact that they behaved as though they believed they were correct.[37] What is significant, then, is that for Tárrega, a slap by a woman, even by a queen, is serious enough to set in motion the events described in the preceding pages, events which led the participants to the brink of death. That such events are unlikely in real life is subordinate in importance.[38]

In *The Inimical Benefactress*, then, Tárrega shows that royalty is not immune to the problems of conjugal honor. Unlike Atila and other protagonists of Virués, Tárrega's king is a God-fearing monarch, aware of the fallaciousness of popular opinion yet bound by it. The king's Christian attitude not only leads to the restoration of his honor through the recovery of his wife's good reputation, but leads as well to the recovery of Laura's honor. Once again, then, as in so many of Tárrega's *comedias*, catastrophe is averted by a brush with death followed by the restoration of honor through mutual forgiveness: "for everything around here is pardon" (I, 621).

VI   La Perseguida Amaltea

Since no man, not even a king, can escape the honor problems that accompany matrimony, it is to be expected that some men would rather not be burdened with such problems. This is the conclusion reached by the count in *La perseguida Amaltea* (Amaltea Pursued), whose marriage to Amaltea is agreed upon early in the drama. However, after becoming involved in what seems to be an inextricable intrigue, the count concludes that marriage is not for him:

> . . . I have thought
> that sacred matrimony
> is a very narrow noose.
> It has caused me agony
> to see its obligations,
> ties, nets, chances,
> displeasure, melancholy.
>
> (I, 327)

Apologizing to Amaltea, he says he cannot marry her, "for I fear that he who takes you away from here will have to bury you." In other words, the count fears that it would not be long before the obligations of the honor code might force him to kill his wife. Bearing in mind Wardropper's previously cited thesis that comedy is to be viewed as a learning process in preparation for the honor problems of married life, it is interesting (and somewhat unusual) that Tárrega suggests in this play that such a learning process may result in the decision not to marry, in view of the mortal dangers involved.

VII   La Sangre Leal de los Montañeses de Navarra

Honor problems in Tárrega's theater are not limited to conjugal conflicts, however, as is evident in *La sangre leal de los montañeses de Navarra* (The Loyal Blood of the Mountaineers of Navarra), considered by some to be Tárrega's masterpiece.[39] Among other things, this play is an inquiry into the nature and origin of honor.

Because the king had taken a liking to Doña Lambra, she, together with her brother Don Fruela and aged father Bermudo, had left their rural birthplace and come to live in the court. When, on one occasion, Doña Lambra resists the amorous advances of the king, the latter reminds her that it was he who had raised her from her village origins to her present position. She, however, responds:

> Notice that in my own place
> I have always had nobility;
> I was a poor vassal,
> I had blood without wealth,
> and your power, in order to honor
>   it [my blood],
> hasn't given me nobility,
> although it gave me something to
>   adorn it with.

The king asks:

> And that is little? More than a thousand
> are noble because of their wealth.

But Doña Lambra objects:

> You gave me estate and advantage,
> you've raised my lineage,
> and thus in my breast you are
> the jeweler who has polished me,
> not the silversmith who has made me.

The king's point of view differs from Doña Lambra's:

> Don't push your honorability;
> for I made that nobility,
> for unseen it was nothing;
> . . . .
> who makes [honors], madam,
> is the one who makes them seen.

Finally, Doña Lambra counters:

> Rather those who are true gentlemen
> suffer those extremes;

> for, since their antiquity
> is much, age could have
> made a change in their luck;
> and note that in rich nobility
> quality is less;
> . . . .
> Bermudo teaches how to live,
> Don Fruela how to fight,
> Doña Lambra how to resist;
> take example from the three.

(I, 346–47)

It is evident that Doña Lambra and the king entertain two diametrically opposed concepts of honor, a fact which is underlined by their respective use of words. Doña Lambra refers to *nobility, blood, lineage, quality* and *antiquity*, words that reflect one's heritage which by itself provides the basis for honor, although it must be maintained by honorable deeds. "Our inherited nobility must be guarded with firmness" (I, 346), she explains. The three ways to preserve this honor are exemplified by Bermudo ("teaches how to live"), whose role as the venerable *paterfamilias* is to hand down the legacy of the family honor by precept and example; Don Fruela ("how to fight"), whose role as the young nobleman is to serve his king in battle; and Doña Lambra herself ("how to resist"), in her role as preserver of the family moral virtue.

The king, on the other hand, speaks only of the external sort of honor whose ultimate source is the king himself. In this sense, he is the creator of nobility and its concomitant honor. The nobility to which Doña Lambra refers and which she claims to have had always "in my own place," did not, according to the king, exist until he made it public by bringing the family to the court (i.e., by honoring them and in this sense giving them honor).

Doña Lambra, of course, does not deny the honor that has been bestowed upon her and her family by the king, but, as she metaphorically points out, he is only the jeweler who has polished her, not the smith who has fashioned her. Doña Lambra's pride in the ancestral blood which she received "without wealth" and her warning that the wealthy nobleman is to be suspected is a reflection of her pride in her pure blood (those who were known as *cristianos viejos* or "old Christians," without taint of Jewish or Moorish blood), for, as she indicates, it is the truly noble family that, because of the many generations it has existed, is likely to have undergone difficult times and lost its fortune. On the other hand, the wealthy family is likely to be of the *noveau riche* class, with its connotation of the recently converted Jew.[40]

While Doña Lambra may take pride in her lineage and confine her concern with honor to the preservation of her chastity, her brother Fruela must concern himself with that other brand of honor which is dependent upon external recognition, despite his awareness that "all honor is appearance" (I, 356). There are times, however, when Fruela wishes that the king had never honored him by bringing him to the court, for now that honor is constantly in danger of being tarnished.[41]

When Fruela is denied entrance to the palace because of an important conference among the king, Bermudo, and Count Anselmo, he is visibly disturbed, because Anselmo and Bermudo had already had one argument stopped by the king on a previous occasion. Fruela's consternation increases when an executioner is brought into the palace. The fear that his father has been offended causes Fruela to curse the day that the king brought him to the court: "Cursed be he who is determined to take the poor from their poverty" (I, 354). If only the king had left him where he found him:

> I wouldn't be as I am
> in this inhuman doubt,
> because of which I blame myself a thousand times;
> for I am not honorable, sister,
> so long as I don't know whether I am.
>
> (I, 355)

We have here, of course, a fundamental difference between the two kinds of honor, external and internal: Doña Lambra was able to contradict the king and without hesitation state that she had inner honor. On the other hand, Don Fruela cannot make a claim to outer honor, for the doubtful circumstances of the moment prevent his knowing whether he has honor and this in itself means that he does not.

Fruela's suspicions are confirmed when he is told by the king that Count Anselmo slapped Bermudo. The king, however, has had the executioner cut off Anselmo's offending hand and considers the matter closed. Proclaiming that honor has been restored, the king asks Fruela to embrace Anselmo. Bermudo, on the other hand, feels that honor has not been restored to him and wants Fruela to avenge him. The problem at hand, then, is whether or not a man's honor is restored by the intervention of the king.

La Du points out that, according to Northup, the answer to the question is yes, in the plays of Calderón, but "it is not equally so in . . . Guillén de Castro."[42] Nor is it so in the theater of Tárrega. Trapped between the command of his king to embrace the offender and the entreaty of his father to kill Anselmo, Fruela obeys them both by embracing the one-handed count so tightly that he suffocates him with "embraces of a gentleman" (I, 356).

The death of Anselmo sets in motion a new series of honor problems. Since the deed was performed in the presence of the king, the latter's honor is involved, and Fruela is sentenced to prison. Significantly, however, the king informs us of his true feelings in an aside: "Has such a noble breast been seen? Although the dishonor is mine, he who has done it to me makes me love" (I, 357).

Fruela's family, of course, is pleased by his deed. "Is there any vengeance so honorable?" asks Doña Lambra, while Bermudo feels rejuvenated:

> since I have recovered my honor,
> from this outrage this blow
> has awakened my blood.
> Now I revive, now I rejuvenate.
>
> (I, 358)[43]

On the other hand, Manfredo, cousin of Anselmo and now the new count, feels that *his* honor has been tarnished: "My lineage is aggrieved" (I, 357), and he vows vengeance. The form that this vengeance takes is treachery in the war, for which he is summarily killed.

I have said that this play deals with the nature and origin of honor. One of the ways in which this comes to light is in the confrontation between the titled family of Anselmo-Manfredo and the untitled *old Christians* of the family of Bermudo-Fruela-Lambra. Not only does the king defend the nobility of Bermudo's lineage as Doña Lambra had defended it to the king, but it is suggested that from the very beginning of the drama that the count's honor, based on his *hombría*, is suspect.

When Anselmo encounters the French warrior Godofre, the former's wagging tongue prompts Godofre to taunt him:

> Don't be, Anselmo, such a talker;
> for he who speaks in battle
> is a trumpet of his own honor,
> and the trumpet does not fight.
>
> (I, 344)

When Anselmo threatens to fight both Godofre and Fruela, Godofre points out that Anselmo really is trying to avoid a fight with either:

> To call two against oneself,
> isn't love, but caution;
> this is the way you want to cover
> the defects of your fame?
> For in order to do and to say,
> he who calls two honorable men,
> doesn't want to quarrel with any.
>
> (I, 344)

A fight does ensue, however, and Godofre deprives Anselmo of his sword and consequently of his honor: "without my sword I cannot approach my king with my honor" (I, 345). After Anselmo's departure, Godofre comments: "He seems a bit courageous but he overflows in speech" (*ibid.*). Manfredo is similarly portrayed as dishonorable, for he considers his personal affairs more important than his loyalty to the king, "because my honor is doubtless worth more than his city" (I, 374).

Tárrega opposes the disloyalty of the counts with the title of the play: *The Loyal Blood of the Mountaineers of Navarra.* It is made clear to the king that he is mistaken in his punishment of Fruela, because the killing of Anselmo was a matter of honor:

> And doesn't it serve as excuse
> his killing him as an honorable man?
> Do you ride roughshod in this
> way over strong men? Then you
> support the conditions of valor badly,
> for men who put up with affronts
> will also put up with treasons.
> He who knows how to guard his honor
> will also know how to guard your city.
>
> (I, 364)

The last two lines clearly contrast Fruela with Manfredo. Of greater significance, however, is the restatement of a conception of honor that was noted earlier in *Reversed Fortunes*, namely, that a man who is willing to defend his honor will likewise live his life in an honorable fashion (i.e., truly be a man of honor).

Unfortunately, however, the king is bound by his concern for his fame: "But the relatives of the dead man will call me a tyrant" (I, 364). The king does not have to resolve the problem for, as has been noted, Manfredo becomes a traitor. Fruela, on the other hand, as well as his father and sister, are instrumental in the victory of the Spaniards, thus in part accounting for the title of this play.

There is yet another aspect to the honor problem and the "loyal blood" of Fruela's family. It is evidently dishonorable for one who is not of royal blood to aspire to a marriage with royalty. Margarita, sister of the king, is in love with Fruela. Doña Lambra fears that her brother reciprocates, but when she learns that he does not, "my brother recovers what he has lost, for in my opinion he just died and then was born" (I, 348). Bermudo also fears that his son may be entertaining hopes of marrying Margarita, in which case it is an affront to him: "This bad son affronts me," as well as a repudiation of his lineage:

> If he has put his thoughts
> in the royal household,
> he is not noble, he is not loyal;
> until I know his intentions
> I shall have to receive him poorly.
>
> (I, 350)

Fruela himself is aware of this and begs Margarita not to pursue her love for him: "Don't destroy me; am I to affront my king by touching things of his?" He admits that he, too, loves Margarita but must forget her "for the sake of being loyal" (I, 360). When, for a brief period of time it appears that the king is dead, Margarita again tries to get Fruela to marry her. Bermudo warns that "a vassal must not become brother-in-law of his lord" (I, 361), and Fruela points out that the death of the king does not relieve one of one's obligations, "for he who does not respect the dead was not truly loyal to the living" (I, 362). Margarita threatens to have Fruela beheaded if he does not agree to marry her, but he still refuses. Bermudo would rather have him die than be dishonored: "Go ahead and cut his throat, for his breast remains pure . . . for the honorable man lives [though] dead" (*ibid.*).

In *Reversed Fortunes*, the old duke had soliloquized that honor or fame survives death; in *The Constant Duchess*, the duke had similarly proclaimed that he did not mind dying, provided that his fame remained, again implying that fame and honor survive death. Here in *Loyal Blood*, Tárrega once more suggests that if one dies with honor, one lives on in the form of that second variety of the life of honor as described by Jorge Manrique.

VIII   El Cerco de Pavía

Situations such as those just described do not depend solely on "what 'they will say' or on what 'they said,'" but belong to those which "are based on an honorable feeling, whose ambience leads to the fame of the characters."[44] How one arrives at such a state is explained in *El cerco de Pavía y prisión del rey de Francia* (The Siege of Pavía and Imprisonment of the King of France), in which Cisneros, having been instrumental in the defeat of the French king, is told that because of his heroism, "with well-known virtue you lose your restful life in order to gain an honorable death" (I, 462). The meaning of these lines is clarified by Cisneros himself when he replies that "rest beckons everyone but work beckons good people" (*ibid.*). In other words, in order to *maintain* one's virtue and *attain* an honorable death, it is necessary to labor. (We are reminded of Doña Lambra's advice in *Loyal Blood*, namely, that the way for the young nobleman to preserve his honor is to fight.) Consequently, it is not enough to be of noble birth, as the marquis explains to General Lanoy:

LANOY: Nature gave me honor
           in the estates of Flanders.
MARQUIS: There are, Lanoy, very great leagues
           between honor and nobility.
           Nobility and valor
           go their separate ways,
           for honor must be young,
           but nobility be old.

                                                              (I, 447)

The last line refers, of course, to the concept of the *old Christian*, described earlier. The penultimate line, however, reaffirms the idea mentioned above, namely, that honor cannot be allowed to grow old but must be rejuvenated by honorable deeds. Not even royalty can content itself with the honor it possesses, for there is always room for more, as the marquis explains on another occasion:

> for in the greatest prince,
> Cisneros, honor always finds
> some empty corner;
> and he who is of good caste
> does what his blood obligates him;
> let him say "enough" to wealth,
> and not say to honor, "It's enough."

(I, 451)

IX *Tárrega: Shadow of Death or Tragicomic Mirror of Life*

In the *comedias* of Tárrega, then, unmarried people must learn to cope with the deceitful nature of life and society while at the same time acknowledging the exigencies of that society, particularly the demands of honor. Because transgression is so often of a comic nature as part of the learning process on the road to more serious states, the shadow of death is often sufficient to lead the characters on the road to moral rectitude. At times the shadow of death may take the form of self-denial; at others, it may be less shadowy and cause people to appear dead;[45] at still other times, actual death befalls a character, if his transgression is serious enough to warrant such a punishment, as in the case of Torcato (*The Constant Duchess*), who had interfered with the divine state of matrimony, or Manfredo (*Loyal Blood*), the traitor.

Furthermore, honor is less questioned in the family of the *old Christian* than in the wealthy and titled nobleman. However, honor cannot be allowed to rest on its own laurels: it is the duty of the elder members of a family to hand down the principles of honor, which are then defended by the youthful male members of the family, while the lady must preserve her honor by constant vigil and resistance. In this manner, the honor attained and preserved leads to fame, not only in its meaning of reputation, but in the form of the "other life," which survives death.

On discussing the death of Atila in the theater of Virués, I had occasion to cite A. A. Parker to the effect that the most severe punishment which the Golden Age drama had to offer is damnation or consignment to hell. No such situation occurs in the theater of Tárrega. Parker goes on to point out that "the next most severe

punishment is death. . . ."[46] It is significant that in the plays of
Tárrega, there is suggested one punishment more severe than death
alone: death without honor or fame. It is interesting to note,
however, that in the three situations in which such a punishment is
suggested (Torcato and Flaminia in *The Constant Duchess* and the
queen in *The Inimical Benefactress*), only the evil Torcato actually
receives this form of castigation. The two women escape this fate
because they were both morally virtuous and the victims of calum-
ny, and in the drama of "seventeenth-century Spain, [it was]
considered fitting that wrongdoing should not go unpunished and
that virtue should not remain unrewarded."[47] In any event, Tárrega
does make it clear that such a death—without honor and without
fame—is, to use a well-worn phrase, a fate worse than death.

Finally, a question raised in the previously cited review by
Fucilla of Froldi's original edition in Italian of 1962, asked, "Has Mr.
Froldi . . . succeeded in vanquishing the myths that have prevailed
about Lope and the creation of the *comedia*?"[48] Over a dozen years
have passed (half a dozen since the Spanish version of Froldi's book)
and only Ebersole, in 1973, cites Froldi as the reason we must not
speak with such exclusivity of a Lope as the single father of the
Spanish *comedia*, adding that the *comedia*, although dominated by
Lope by the beginning of the seventeenth century, is the result of
an evolutionary process which flourished as much in Valencia as in
Seville and Madrid, perhaps more oriented toward the new forms in
Valencia than in the other centers. This is why, says Fucilla, he
includes Tárrega in his anthology.[49] A lonely tribute, considering
the number of books, many of them already cited here, such as
those of Aubrun, A. Castro, Crawford (the revised edition), López
Morales, and others (such as Margaret Wilson's *Spanish Drama of
the Golden Age*, 1969; Sturgis E. Leavitt's *An Introduction to Golden Age Drama in Spain*, 1971; and Everett Hesse and Juan Valencia's *El teatro anterior a Lope de Vega*, 1971), which do not even
mention Tárrega. This chapter, as well as Froldi's book, although
they often represent differing interpretations and give different
weight to the various works, are sufficient reason to give major
attention to the role of Canon Tárrega in the development of the
Spanish *comedia*.

CHAPTER 5

Aguilar

"THE most important dramatist of the Valencian group, after Guillén de Castro, is, without doubt, Gaspar de Aguilar."[1] Born in Valencia, Aguilar was baptized there on January 14, 1561.

On April 16, 1587, the poet married Luisa Peralta, daughter of a tailor. Martí Grajales maintains that this marriage was contracted against the wishes of Gaspar's father, who, it is said, disinherited the dramatist and thus set in motion a series of misfortunes which plagued Gaspar until his death.[2] Mérimée, on the other hand, considers the cause of Aguilar's misfortunes to be a combination of law suits incurred by his father and the large number of children that the poet had.[3]

Aguilar was one of the founding members of the *Academia de los Nocturnos*, in which he participated under the pseudonym of *Sombra* ("Shadow"). Many of his contemporaries wrote laudatory comments about him, among them Lope de Vega, Cervantes, Artieda, Beneyto, and Tárrega.[4] The poet died on July 25, 1623, and was buried on the following day.

I La Gitana Melancólica

Artieda, Virués, and Tárrega showed that honor is not attained through death alone. This conception is also present in Aguilar's *La gitana melancólica* (The Melancholy Gypsy).[5]

After Jerusalem has been surrounded by the Romans, the Jewish leaders decide that their only hope lies in the death of the Roman emperor. Accordingly, it is decided that Aber, daughter of the Jewish general, Josefo, is to go to the emperor, make him fall in love with her, and then kill him. If she accomplishes this, her father tells her, "in the books of fame shall your name be written" (II, 18). Aber agrees with this interpretation, for when Unías, her fiancé, begs her not to go through with the assassination, she replies that she must or

else "the glory that results for me remains hidden" (II, 20). Learning
that it was not the emperor but one of his deputies whom she has
killed, Aber asks for death:

> Give me a death so full
> of rigor that it astonish the world;
> because my fortune ordains
> that, since I didn't eternalize my name,
> I can eternalize my pain.
>
> (II, 26)

In other words, Aber seeks a painful death which will underline her
failure. Her desire for punishment is indicative of the fact that for
those who are failures there can be no fame. The emperor, however,
is so impressed by the valor of Aber's deed that he decides to give
freedom to Jerusalem, causing Aber to be proud of her hand which
"has been able to give you life by erring" (II, 27), for had she not
killed the wrong man, the emperor would not be alive now to end
the siege, nor would he have any reason to do so.

Unías does not share the emperor's opinion, for he believes that
such fame is reserved for men alone, "for killing is a male's [way] to
earn eternal name" (II, 32). On the other hand, if this is not possible, one should die in a glorious manner. This explains why Unías,
when confronted by one of the most illustrious Roman soldiers and
asked why he chooses to fight such a well-known warrior, responds
that "I die in order to die in good hands" (II, 31). Consequently,
Unías feels that death alone is not sufficient to bestow fame: if he
cannot "earn eternal name" through his conquests, then he sees the
possibility of achieving it by dying in combat at the hands of a
famous soldier.

Events have caused the emperor to change his mind and resume
the siege, the nature of which is such that all hope seems lost for
Jerusalem. Accordingly, Josefo feels that death is preferable to
captivity and plans not only to commit suicide but to perform "the
greatest deed which any man has done," which is to kill Aber and
Unías:

> Let me, then, lord, give them death;
> What do I mean death? Eternal and holy life,
> for with it I free and rescue them
> from the hard, intolerable captivity.
>
> (II, 33)

For Josefo, the ignominy of captivity makes death equivalent to life, nay, more than life, for it is the means to a holy and eternal existence.

Before attempting the deaths of Aber and Unías, Josefo wishes them to be married "so as to kill only one." Despite the circumstances, Unías considers this to be "the lucky day which I so cheerfully awaited" and asks Aber to marry him. Aber promises to be his wife, but Unías answers that he gives her his "word that I am and not that I shall be."[6]

Josefo does not go through with the killing, however, for the Roman emperor explains to him not only that he would not make slaves of people of noble blood (i.e., dishonor them) but that it is wrong for Josefo to shed that blood. In short, the Christian attitude prevails.

Interestingly, when the situation was reversed, Josefo's attitude was similar to the emperor's. When the Roman hero, Numa, had been captured by the Jewish soldiers, the latter were about to kill him because Numa had killed so many Jews in battle. Josefo had spared Numa's life, pointing out that Numa was "obligated to fight" and thus "does not deserve punishment" and that consequently, the Jewish soldiers had no motive for considering Numa's actions as an affront, "for there is never thirst for vengeance where there is no fire of insult" (II, 7).

Before Josefo's intervention, Numa had told the Jews who were about to kill him that he did not mind dying, provided that someone ensured his fame by publicizing the fact that he was outnumbered: "in order for my name not to die, let there be among so many one man to say that you were so many" (II, 7). Such fame, obtained through one's adversaries, is the highest one can aspire to, "for when fame comes out of the opponent's mouth, it is that much more publicized and spread" (II, 13).

II Los Amantes de Cartago

Another play in which a siege occurs is *Los amantes de Cartago* (The Lovers of Carthage), but the glories obtained in battle serve only as a background for the more important aspects. This play opens with a scene reminiscent of one which I quoted at length from Tárrega's *The Inimical Benefactress*. Siface, king of Sirta, is asked why he is so unhappy. After he denies several possible causes suggested by his servant, the latter wonders, "What sharper ailment is there than love, death, rage, or grief?" Siface replies, "A glory put in doubt" (II, 85).

Once more we see that even kings are dependent on what others think. As the servant says, "Great patience is needed if such a well-developed glory is in doubt." The problem facing Siface is that the Carthaginian senate is deciding whether he or Macinisa, king of Numiaia, is to rule Carthage and marry Sofonisba. When the senate chooses Macinisa, Siface's first reaction is to long for death, in view of his loss of honor; on second thought, he considers his loss of honor to mean that he is already dead: "Don't say . . . that I shall die nor that I'm dying, but that I'm dead already" (II, 86). Subsequently, however, Siface decides to take power by force. When Macinisa, who had hoped to gain fame as a result of the senate's decision— "More than life I want that glory to aggrandize me" (II, 87–88)— hears that the people have accepted Siface as their king, his reaction is the same as that of Siface had been: "I'm dead." The senate now refuses to allow Macinisa to proceed with his wedding to Sofonisba. When he asks them what he is lacking, they reply, "Name, fame, majesty, wealth, honor, towns, villages, cities" (II, 90). Thus it is established that even a king has honor and fame only so long as others acknowledge these qualities. Once honor is lost, the king considers himself dead. This conception is reinforced when Macinisa meets Cipión, the Roman general who has come to invade Carthage. Macinisa insists that he is not a man, for "an unfortunate one isn't a man." As Macinisa raves on about his desire for death, Cipión's captain remarks that Macinisa "seems in his thoughts to be a man of quality" (II, 94). In other words, only men of nobility would react in accordance with the conception of honor described above.

Joining forces with Cipión, Macinisa decides it is his turn to employ force. After seriously wounding Siface, he attempts to re-gain Sofonisba, who, in the meantime, had married Siface. Despite the fact that Sofonisba loves Macinisa, she rejects his amorous advances until news is received that Siface has died of his wounds. Then, however, she tells Macinisa that his good fortune is reborn because of this death, explaining that "now I am mine" and that she had turned away his previous advances "for the sake of seeming well" (II, 101). In other words, while her husband was alive, honor demanded fidelity from her, but the moment he was dead, Sofonisba belonged to herself once more. Not only can she now accept Macinisa's advances but she herself suggests that they marry.

Thus then and there, only moments after the news of her husband's death is received, Sofonisba promises her hand in marriage to Macinisa, the two agreeing to keep the marriage secret.[7]

Cipión, however, also wishes to make love to Sofonisba, who finds that the only way to maintain her honor is to reveal the clandestine marriage. Cipión's first reaction is to want to eliminate Macinisa, but military concerns require the latter's allegiance, so that Cipión decides upon Sofonisba's death instead. He also decides that Macinisa should be the one to kill her. Since Macinisa considers Cipión's advances to Sofonisba an affront to his honor as a husband, he considers himself obligated to kill her. Not only would he remove the stain upon his own honor through the death of his wife but he believes that this death will purify Sofonisba, preserve her reputation, and, in so doing, overcome physical death. Accordingly, he hopes that her rosy light will:

> not withdraw and leave your cheeks
> deadened, wan, and yellow;
> it is better to give a sign
> of your divine rather than human breast,
> and by making a sacrifice
> try with happy, cheerful face,
> to the sovereign heavens
> to lift your hardship with incense,
> and let the smoke-turned tongue repeat it.
>
> (II, 113)

Macinisa believes that, by killing Sofonisba, he is providing her with a triumphant death, a sacrifice which overcomes the physical decay of death through the fame (her "smoke-turned tongue") which accompanies it. Of course, Macinisa also believes that his own dishonor would be erased, since his honor depends upon her fame or reputation. The captain who brings the poisonous drink also believes that Macinisa "is trying to achieve a death which will never end" (II, 114), and Sofonisba herself welcomes "this fortunate luck to which heaven invites me, because what I leave is death; and what I receive is life," because "only death can make me immortal" (II, 115).

Cipión changes his mind, however, and decides that Macinisa and Sofonisba may live together. (He has not yet heard of the poisoning.) Aguilar then follows Tárrega's device of revealing that Sofonisba had only been touched by the shadow of death, for she had drunk only a potion to make her appear dead. Although both Macinisa and Sofonisba may have felt that death was justifiable, God evidently did not, for "The permission/of Heaven, which is powerful, moved my heart/by seeing your wife die with such little cause" (II, 120). The speaker of these lines is the man to whom Macinisa had entrusted the manufacture of the poison, but as he points out, the will of Heaven "had such power" that he prepared a harmless potion instead.[8] The reason that Sofonisba's fate is no more than a brush with the shadow of death is, of course, that she had maintained honor and virtue by her own behavior in resisting Cipión.

III   La Venganza Honrosa

Such is not the case, however, in *La venganza honrosa* (Honorable Vengeance), in which Porcia, although married to Duke Norandino, is in love with Duke Astolfo and plans to run away with the latter, being content "to close my eyes to my honor" (II, 339).

When news is received that Porcia has fled with Astolfo, there occurs a brief discussion between Norandino and the duke of Mantua, Porcia's father. The two men argue about who is to avenge the dishonor. Despite his age, the duke feels it is his obligation to kill Porcia and Astolfo, "for I am the root whence your affront came forth" (II, 344). But, of course, once a lady is married, it is the husband, not the father, who is responsible for her actions. Moreover, it would be an affront to the husband were the father to take upon himself the vengeance of the dishonor, as Norandino makes clear to the duke:

> You're going to go looking for Porcia?
> What's this? Am I not alive?
> Don't you see that you will offend me
> much more by following her
> than she offended me by leaving?
>
> (II, 344)

Norandino must be the one to avenge the dishonor not only because of his responsibility as the husband, but as a result of a more general requirement of the honor code, namely, that the offended man himself must avenge the dishonor. Were someone else to do it for him, the dishonor would still remain. Accordingly, when the old duke asks who is to take vengeance, Norandino replies:

> He to whom the offense was made:
> and so it must only be I
> who can kill my wife;
> for the man who has need
> of another to kill her for him, remains
> with the affront and without a wife.
>
> (II, 345)

It is significant that this discussion ends in a definitive statement, since the dishonor in *Honorable Vengeance* is very real, for a similar argument in Tárrega's *The Inimical Benefactress* was left unresolved, inasmuch as the dishonor was subsequently shown not to have existed. Consequently, Norandino kills both Porcia and Astolfo, a deed that wins the approval of the old duke.

For Mérimée (p. 501) the chief idea contained in *Honorable Vengeance* is the punishment which faces an adulterous wife. I cannot deny this obvious message in the denouement of the play, but it appears to me that there is more involved here. Mérimée's translation of the title as *L'honneur vengé* (Avenged Honor) compared to my own *Honorable Vengeance* is indicative of our divergent points of view, for his rendition causes us to concentrate, as he indeed did, on the denouement. But Aguilar's title, *La venganza honrosa*, does not emphasize an outcome; the subject is not honor avenged. The title of the play stresses vengeance, and the adjective *honrosa* reveals the nature of that vengeance. I am not, I think, quibbling with words here, for, while this play may indeed have as its moral the punishment that awaits the adulterous wife, it has as its theme the honorable *manner* in which this punishment is to be administered.

Part of that manner has already been revealed in the discussion between Norandino and the old duke. Another aspect of it appears when Norandino is thought to be dead. Norandino's ambassador, believing that his lord had died before being able to take vengeance on Porcia, asks, "What about the deceased, in whom are honor's remains, which, he being dead, will leave with him?" (II, 357). In other words, had Norandino really died without avenging the dishonor brought upon him, his death would not have erased that dishonor. But the death of Porcia at the hands of her husband does erase his dishonor. What is more, Porcia herself recovers her fame through her death according to her father, who only now calls her "daughter":

My daughter, and don't be surprised
by this name which I have given you,
for since you paid for your sin,
you can well recover your name.

(II, 373)

The full significance of the above becomes clearer when we compare
Honorable Vengeance and *The Lovers of Carthage*, whereupon it
becomes even more difficult to accept Mérimée's assessment of
these matters as a pitiless thesis. In *The Lovers of Carthage*, Aguilar
presented the possibility that death erases dishonor, but there was
no death, for the wife has preserved her honor by resisting the
advances of her oppressor. Since the dishonor was based on a
shadow of the truth (suspicion), merely the shadow of death and not
actual death was sufficient to restore that honor. The prevention of
actual death was thus described as a reflection of the will of God.

On the other hand, in *Honorable Vengeance* the dishonor is not
merely suspected; it is real and it is known by the peoples of two
dukedoms. Consequently, the death which serves to erase that
dishonor must likewise be real. In this play, the concept that death
alone erases dishonor is qualified by several conditions. The death of
the adultress at the hands of her father would not restore honor to
her husband; nor would the death of the husband restore that hon-
or. What is required is the death of the offender at the hands of the
offended. Therefore, although it may appear that death alone erases
dishonor, such is not the case. The restoration of honor is attained
through death but according to certain principles of the honor code.
Hence, honor-restoring vengeance, or *Honorable Vengeance*.

Froldi (p. 132) also rejects Mérimée's analysis, as does Bershas,
who, in an interesting attempt to find national source material for
this play, concludes that *La venganza honrosa* "must be accounted
an interesting, if not completely successful, attempt at what Lope
was to achieve so well, the utilization of epic and chronicle sources
for the *comedia*."[9]

IV   La Suerte sin Esperanza

The manner, and not simply the fact, of the retention and recovery of honor is thus a prime concern for Aguilar. Accordingly, even
King Ferdinand the Catholic must recognize a man's need to avenge
himself in *La suerte sin esperanza* (Hopeless Luck). In this play
Aguilar shows that not even at the hands of the law does death
restore lost honor.

Having fallen from his horse and hurt himself, Lamberto is given lodging at the home of Mauricio, whose sister arouses the passion of their guest. Since such an affair would be contrary to the laws of hospitality, the mere suspicion of it is an insult to Mauricio, "for suspicion left unascertained is an affront (II, 210). To avoid a duel and satisfy Mauricio's desire to maintain honor, Lamberto promises to marry Leonarda (Mauricio's sister), and the young couple exchange marriage promises. However, Lamberto already has a wife, a fact which he does not reveal to Leonarda until they are well on their way to his home in Valencia. Leonarda persuades him to introduce her as a slave, and in these circumstances she actually lives with Lamberto and his wife for a period of years!

In the meantime, Mauricio had become involved in an honor affair of his own. Although little is said of this, it does become evident that Mauricio had insulted a certain Don Alonso, who had demanded a duel in order to recover his honor. Arriving for the duel, Mauricio found not Alonso but a servant with a letter informing him that Alonso had called off the duel in view of the fact that Mauricio was without honor and consequently could not give to Alonso what he, Mauricio, did not have. This digression provides another example of which sort of death does not restore honor. To the concepts garnered from the previously analyzed works can be added that even though the offender meets death at the hands of the offended one himself, the latter does not recover his honor if the former is without any.

The reason for Mauricio's dishonor is, of course, that someone has discovered that his sister Leonarda was "married" to a man who already had a wife. Consequently, Mauricio goes to Valencia determined to kill Leonarda and Lamberto but arrives just in time to witness Lamberto stab Leonarda as punishment for having recently revealed her true identity to Lamberto's wife. This changes Mauricio's mission: having come to kill Leonarda, he now finds himself obligated to avenge her death. Fortunately, however, the wound is not fatal, but no one else knows it, so that Leonarda is thought to be dead. But Mauricio must avenge the attempted murder as well as the previous affront of Lamberto. Leonarda points out to her brother that it is not up to him to administer justice, but that if it is his honor that he wishes to avenge, then he must challenge Lamberto to a duel, "because justice, brother, doesn't avenge, but [only] punish" (II, 237).[10] She advises Mauricio to go to King Ferdinand, who is visiting Valencia, and remind the king that although Lamberto has been sentenced to death, Mauricio's honor will not be satisfied because "through justice an honorable man is not avenged."

Accordingly, Mauricio goes to the king and asks him not to allow Lamberto to be executed, for vengeance by another's hand, even though it be the hand of the law, is not really vengeance but only punishment and therefore does not erase dishonor. On the other hand, if Mauricio is given a chance to kill Lamberto in a duel, "My name will rise to heaven, my fame will remain eternal" (II, 238). What is more, the effort alone will ensure his honor even if he loses the duel: "I will consider myself the victor even if Lamberto defeats me" (II, 239).

King Ferdinand agrees with this concept and grants Mauricio permission to challenge Lamberto:

> Since you esteem honor so much,
> it is well that it thank you
> for the great faith you have in it
>
> . . . .
>
> and thus, although it might be better
> to execute the sentence,
> because, after all, punishment
> removes obligation, even if it doesn't avenge,
>
> . . . .
>
> I give you, Mauricio, permission.
>
> (II, 238)

It is noteworthy that in the eyes of the king it might be better to let justice run its course, because even though punishment does not avenge, it does remove the obligation for vengeance. More significant, however, is that the king does not let this prevent Mauricio from seeking revenge. Consequently, even the king recognizes the need of an honorable man to take vengeance.

It is surely not by mere chance that Aguilar chose for the king of his play the man who is universally known as Ferdinand the Catholic, for, in so doing, he arrives at a synthesis between the honor code and Christianity. As I mentioned in chapter 4, it was a belief inherited from the Goths that the outcome of a duel represented the judgment of God. Consequently, the duel in this play satisfies the exigencies of the offended, of the offender, of the honor code, and of Christianity. The fact that the duel is not concluded (Leonarda appears at the last moment) does not invalidate the satisfaction of these demands, "for each one has been honorable on this occasion" (II, 243). What is more, since the Council of Trent had recently condemned the custom of the duel, Aguilar's success in synthesizing Christian and pagan ethics is masterful.

But there is yet another dimension to this *comedia* which must be considered. Throughout this study I have been dealing primarily with the Valencian dramatists as precursors of Lope de Vega. There is an element in *Hopeless Luck* which is perhaps more important to Calderonian than to Lopean studies.

When, as the play opens, Lamberto falls from his horse, there occurs a brief discussion among three unnamed characters, who, although offstage, have their words intertwined with the principal dialogue between Mauricio and Leonarda. While brother and sister are discussing trivialities, one of the anonymous bystanders (although addressing what he believes to be the moribund Lamberto), interrupts the dialogue between Mauricio and Leonarda to say, "To God, sir, commend thyself" (II, 206). We may interpret this, in light of the development of the drama, as either a warning to Lamberto to beware of God's judgment or an interpolated piece of advice to Mauricio to leave matters in God's hands. In view of my interpretation of this work, I must conclude that this opening scene confirms Aguilar's attempt to reach a synthesis between Christian and pagan ethics. From the audience's point of view, *both* men are given notice to heed the will of God.

Furthermore, the imagery employed by Aguilar, namely Lamberto's inability to control his horse, is a revelation of his failure to control his animal (i.e., sexual) instincts and provides us, in the very first scene, with an insight into Lamberto's character and its basic flaw, namely, his inability to restrain his passion. (It is interesting to note that in a subsequent scene a few moments later, Lamberto's servant tells him that passion is the beginning of madness, a reflection of Aguilar's use of a typical *comedia* device in two ways: the servant making observations of wisdom and the use of aphorisms to point up the specific elements of a given play.) The horse and rider metaphor is not, of course, original with Aguilar, but its use here (as well as that of other elements) helps to place this Valencian in the mainstream of a long tradition which finds its most frequent use in Calderón. Valbuena Briones gives a concise summary of the evolution of the theme, although he does not mention Aguilar.[11]

The opening scenes, therefore, reveal Aguilar's artistry. Combining the action of the rider's fall from his horse with the dialogue of triviality interspersed with the warning to heed God and the linking of passion with madness or foolishness, Aguilar at once uncovers Lamberto's baser instincts, warns him of God's judgment, and simultaneously warns Mauricio of the same thing, thus preparing the way for the resolution and the role played by King Ferdinand. I should add that the dramatic irony contained in the lines referring to passion and God is heightened by Mauricio's words following Lamberto's fall. At that time, there is doubt whether Lamberto is dead or unconscious, and Mauricio pronounces that he will either cure or bury Lamberto. At this stage of the action, the words appear to have only their literal sense, but when viewed in the context of the need to be cured from the madness of passion and Mauricio's insistence on exacting vengeance, these lines show the care with which Aguilar was capable of putting his plays together.

With regard to the honor code, *Hopeless Luck* adds two corollaries to what has been said previously: not only must the offended man himself take vengeance but the offender must be a man of honor. That is to say, the offender must have satisfied any previous attacks upon *his* honor, for so long as a slur upon his name remains unchallenged or unsatisfied (i.e., he has not demonstrated his *hombría*), he is not worthy of a new challenge. Furthermore, although the punishment of the offender by justice alone theoretically removes the obligation of the offended, this concept is not followed, for in the mind of the offended one, justice delivers punishment to the offender but not vengeance to the aggrieved. It is also important to note that the manly effort to undertake a duel is more significant for honor than is the outcome. Finally, *Hopeless Luck* serves as an excellent example of Aguilar's art and craftsmanship, as revealed in his use of imagery, dialogue, and development of scenes.

V   El Mercader Amante

What am I to say, then, of the duel which serves as the opening scene for *El mercader amante* (The Loving Merchant)? The two men are squires, that is, representatives of the nobility, but neither is certain of the reason for the duel: "Afterward we'll find out why we are killing each other" (II, 125). Yet each is very careful not to harm the other and when Astolfo, servant of Belisario, happens to pass by (i.e., their *hombría* has been noticed) and asks them to sheathe their swords, they do so immediately, causing Astolfo to comment that "you are tempering your flames at the cost of your fames" (II, 126). Not long after this, Astolfo relates the event to his master, recounting how badly the two squires had fought, for every move was forecast so that each man knew beforehand of the moves of the other. Consequently, had Astolfo not interrupted the fight, neither of the two men would have been hurt anyway. The significance of this opening scene becomes clear when viewed in the context of the principal action of the play.

Labinia and Lidora are both in love with the merchant Belisario, the wealthiest man of the town. Don Garcia, a nobleman who is in love with Labinia, warns her that despite Belisario's wealth—or more precisely, because of it—the merchant's lineage is suspect: "so poor of lineage that he descends from himself" (II, 129). To Labinia's father, D. García points out that so many fathers are so preoccupied with arranging marriages for their daughters to men of means that in so doing they deprive their grandchildren of pure, noble blood (II, 134).

Aguilar thus presents a theme discussed in the works of Tárrega: the newly rich are suspect because it is likely that they are not *old Christians*. Labinia, however, defends Belisario, for to her a man's character is of primary importance: if he is wealthy, too, his riches should be considered an embellishment rather than a disparagement (II, 129).[12]

Lidora, on the other hand, is presented with a less subtle denunciation of Belisario by the old squire Loaisa, who tells her that Belisario gave him lunch that day and, among other things, the merchant served him "some slices of bacon because he [Belisario] wouldn't eat them" (II, 132). To the implication that Belisario is of Jewish descent, because he will not eat bacon, Lidora reacts by first chiding Loaisa for his malicious tongue and subsequently agreeing that such a conclusion is perfectly normal in view of Belisario's wealth:

> Is that what you say, wicked tongue?
> . . . .
> But there's no reason for me to be surprised;
> for to be rich is [only] a trapping
> for a man to be a Christian,
> and to be rich is not a good name
> in order to be an old Christian.   (II, 132)

Belisario and his servant Astolfo are unaware of this gossip, however, for as the latter explains to his master, Lidora and Labinia "want to marry you because, without your estate, you give evidence of your lineage" (II,127). Belisario wants to learn which of the two women would continue to love him if he were not wealthy. Accordingly, he pretends to lose his fortune while at the same time instructing Astolfo to pretend to have acquired one.

Astolfo's new status as a man of means causes Lidora to prefer him over the now apparently poor Belisardo. Moreover, the father of Labinia now favors the marriage proposal of Garcia. To protect the interests of his master, the loyal Astolfo pretends to want to marry Labinia, knowing that her father will again prefer wealth to nobility and thus ignore Garcia. The latter finds himself compelled to defend his noble lineage against yet another *nouveau riche:* "You haven't been rich long and I have been noble for a long time," to which Astolfo replies:

> if the son of someone [*hijodalgo*][13] is good
> then the father of someone is better:
> for the father engenders the fame
> of all his descendence,
> and in the end greater preeminence
> belongs to the trunk than the branch.

>   (II, 158)

For Astolfo, then, the founder of a lineage is its source of fame and consequently is of higher esteem than his descendents.[14] What is more, Astolfo believes that wealth can produce nobility because it is a syrup which purifies blood (II, 151).

Now I can return to the opening scene of this drama, in which the parody of an honor duel presents two *old Christians* in an apparent attempt to defend their honor at the risk of death. An empty gesture, a feigned attempt to defend one's honor in order to satisfy the demands of public opinion: this is how *old Christians* react when put to the test. Once their so-called *hombría* has been publicly noticed, there need be no fight to the finish, and, although they believe that they have demonstrated that honor is more important than life itself, the folly of their reasoning is revealed in Astolfo's comment that by halting the duel they are expunging the flames of their ire at the cost of their fame.

With such a scene as an overture, Aguilar leads us to favor not the *old Christian* but the merchant Belisario, a "self-made man," in a sense much more literal than that which we tend to attach to it today, for Belisario is a man "who descends from himself."

If, then, the duel between the two squires shows the folly of risking death for the sake of honor based upon external recognition, the plot of Belisario to feign poverty presents a value of greater worth: love. Although Lidora foresakes Belisario when she is led to believe that he has lost his fortune, Labinia continues to love him. When her father orders her to marry García, Labinia says she would rather die. This is no idle metaphor; Labinia literally prefers death to an undesired marriage. Aware of the seriousness of Labinia's threat, her father tells her that if she does not marry García, he will kill her. Labinia still refuses to accede to her father's wishes "because death greatly ennobles a strong breast" (II, 148).

In the meantime, the father has learned of the newly acquired wealth of Astolfo and now orders Labinia to marry Astolfo. Once again, Labinia prefers death to an unwanted marriage: "for it will be a sweet fortune for me to be dead and not married" (II, 155). It is of significance that the words employed by Labinia on these occasions (*ennobles, strong breast, sweet fortune*) are the same as those which heretofore we have seen in connection with matters of honor and *hombría*. The parallel does not end here; just as the man concerned with his honor had learned that death itself does not guarantee the retention or restoration of honor, so Labinia becomes aware that her death at the hands of her father would not accomplish anything. Since for her, the constancy of her love is the equivalent of the *caballero*'s goal of honor, the death required is that of her "enemy," that is, the man who would marry her against her will. She therefore resolves to kill Astolfo by pretending to agree to the marriage. In this way, she plans to stab Astolfo or kill herself in the attempt, but even in the latter case, the circumstances of her death will preserve the love she feels for Belisario. The language of the *caballero* continues:

> What laurel or what palm do I gain
> by suffering the punishment,
> if I don't take with my own hand
> vengeance on an enemy?
> So that it may not be a mistake
> to suffer this torment,

it is better, in such combat,
to make of my thought
a Samson who should die or kill.

. . . .

I'll give death to my opponent
and preserve the faith
which I owe to Belisario.

(II, 155)

Later in an aside, Labinia speaks of the possibility of a martyrdom
"which fame will proclaim with funereal sound" (II, 156), reaffirm-
ing that if she cannot kill her unloved partner in the marriage
ceremony, she will kill herself (cf. the Samson analogy above).

Thus death for the sake of love, like death for the sake of honor,
may lead to fame. Death alone, however, is not sufficient, as we
have seen, and, accordingly, death at the hands of her father would
be a punishment for Labinia, but no more than that. What is required is death—that of the unloved suitor or her own—at the
wedding ceremony.

VI   Aguilar's Works: The Beginnings of Honor Codification

In the plays of Gaspar de Aguilar, dishonor must be avenged by
the offended man himself; the offender must himself not be a
dishonored man, for such a man is in no position to return what he
does not possess. The death of the offended person prior to vengeance does not erase the offense and hence does not restore lost
honor. The castigation of the offender by the law removes the obligation on the part of the offended; nevertheless, it does not provide vengeance nor does it restore honor. In these matters Aguilar
is, of course, adhering to conventional concepts of the *comedia*.

Like honor, love may be the motivating force which causes a
person to prefer death to its loss. In *The Loving Merchant*, the
woman in love, like the man of honor, achieves fame by dem-
onstrating her constancy with an act at the wedding ceremony (her
battlefield), rather than simply accepting the punishment from her
father (the law). In *The Lovers of Carthage*, Aguilar presents the
concept that death erases the dishonor of a husband whose reputation had been stained through the apparently unvirtuous behavior of
his wife. Since the dishonor was subsequently found not to have
existed, however, the death similarly was not realized, a situation
interpreted as the intervention of God. In *The Melancholy Gypsy*, it

is indicated that Aber will obtain eternal fame if she kills the Roman emperor. Her failure to do so (since she unwittingly kills the wrong man) is considered indicative of her failure to obtain fame. Consequently, her request for punishment in the form of an inglorious death again reveals that death alone does not provide fame. It is the bestowing of liberty (through the emperor's death, which presumably would have put an end to the siege of Jerusalem) which provides that fame. Such an attitude is similarly displayed by Aber's father when he plans to kill Aber, Unias, and himself in order to avoid enslavement and thus achieve "eternal and holy life." In each of these instances, fame takes on a different character. In Aber's case, it is simply fame and in Josefo's case it has a twofold nature: first, the evasion of ignominy (enslavement) and second, the afterlife, in the form of peaceful release. In both cases, however, fame is dependent upon the achievement of liberty.

Finally, Aguilar has presented some enlightening aspects of the attitude of the *old Christian*. The latter's position may be presented approvingly, as for example, in the case of Mauricio (*Hopeless Luck*), who receives the consent of King Ferdinand the Catholic to gain fame (i.e., preserve his reputation by recovering his honor) in a duel, irrespective of the outcome. More accurately, the virile attempt to recover honor by undertaking a duel is sufficient to reveal the manly sense of honor, while the absence of the consummation of a duel follows Christian doctrine. *Hopeless Luck*, then, achieves the rare synthesis of Christian and pagan ethical values, a fact reinforced by King Ferdinand's role in the play. The attitude of the *old Christian* may also be presented facetiously, as in the case of the two squires in *The Loving Merchant*, who similarly participate in a duel until they have been noticed (i.e., until their alleged *hombría* has been noticed), without regard for the outcome.

As Froldi observes (p. 133), Aguilar is not dependent on the Lopean theater although he remains close to Lope by virtue of a community of ideals and of principles, all of which confirms the existence in Valencia of a highly lively theatrical tradition when Lope de Vega first arrived in 1588.

CHAPTER 6

Beneyto

W E know very little of the biography of the Valencian poet Miguel Beneyto, which may be ascribed in part to the fact that all that remains of his literary production is a scattering of poems and one *comedia*. Moreover, as Martí Grajales points out, there were several personalities with the same name as the poet in the latter half of the sixteenth century, which has made it difficult to distinguish our poet from others of the same name.[1]

Beneyto was probably born during the early 1560s and died at a young age in October, 1599. He was a charter member of the *Academia de los Nocturnos* under the pseudonym of *Sosiego* ("Serenity"). It appears that Beneyto wrote several plays, but the only one that was actually published, *El hijo obediente* (The Obedient Son), has not been well received by the critics. Mesonero Romanos, for example, does not consider it worth including in his edition of representative plays by the Valencian dramatists.

Mérimée (p. 636) concludes that *The Obedient Son* is a wise, correct, and deliberate work, which lacks only inspiration! Juliá finds Beneyto's dramaturgy a step backward, representing the concerns immediately subsequent to the art of Virués. *The Obedient Son*, he maintains, corresponds to the kind of early works of Guillén de Castro, and is closer to Tárrega's system than to that of Aguilar (p. cxxvi). Froldi (p. 134) considers the work disorganized and lacking deep dramatic motifs but nonetheless typical of the predominant taste in Valencia around the end of the century.

As the title suggests, the plot of this play revolves around the desire of León, son of the emperor, to place obedience to his father above all else. As the play begins, it is made clear that the emperor received his title only by marriage to the daughter of the former emperor. Since she is dead, the emperor is ruling only until León comes of age. It is at this point that the action of the drama begins.

León's ascent to the throne is, of course, a rise in stature for him. Conversely, this event represents a decrease in stature for the emperor, who now bemoans his loss of prestige and feels that León is figuratively killing him. The emperor is therefore ready to accept the advice of the traitor Mauricio to have León put to death.

However, a surprising thing occurs at the coronation ceremony. After the emperor crowns León, the latter returns the crown:

> and thus I wish to return,
> so that you may be my heir,
> the being I came to have,
> and be the first son,
> that gave being to his father.
>
> (II, 383)

León, by returning the crown, returns his power and social status and thereby metaphorically gives existence to his own father. Apologizing to the emperor for having held the crown for even so short a time, León explains that "since I wished to honor myself, I waited for it to be mine in order to be able to give it to you" (II, 383). The concept of honor contained in this quotation is, of course, simply that of paying respect. In order to bestow respect upon the emperor, León evidently felt it necessary first to obtain a token of that respect (the crown), which he subsequently was able to return to his father.

The emperor now wishes to reward León for his action and commands the people to spread the news: "Have this deed live through the mouths of people. . . . Some of you lend wings and tongue to fame," to which the people respond, "Let fame fly to tell it with more tongue and more wings" (II, 383). This kind of fame—or more accurately, *Fame*—is the classical personification of public report, pictured with wings in order to go about quickly to spread news of deeds such as the loyal act of León.

However, León does not wish to be honored, for he considers it wrong for any part of the honors to go to him:

> because the honor which you give me,
> you owe to my father:
> note that you affront me,
> if the deed that you extol
> you pay with praise,
> for I don't want any payment.
>
> (II, 383–84)

Here indeed is an interpretation of honor that we have not come upon before. Because he is obsessed with his desire to be an obedient son, León feels that it is his duty to protect the honor of his father. Therefore, if the people wish to honor him, he believes that he is receiving honor which rightfully belongs to his father. According to this line of reasoning, then, the bestowing of honor upon León is nothing less than an affront to León, since it interferes with his duty of looking out for his father's honor!

That León is truly obsessed with his desire to protect his father's honor is revealed in his next meeting with the emperor. The latter, urged on by the traitor Mauricio, fears that León may change his mind and demand the crown once again. (Mauricio also falsely tells the emperor that León has amorous designs on the woman with whom the emperor is in love.) Consequently, the emperor persists in his original plan to have his son killed.

León is summoned to appear before the emperor. Realizing that the emperor wishes to kill him, León does not resist. On the contrary, he suggests that he be killed secretly so that his father will not gain a bad reputation. León does not mind dying if that is his father's wish, but he will feel anguish if his death deprives the emperor of his fame. In fact, his reference to himself as an innocent lamb (II, 387) is not self-pity. Rather, he wishes he were guilty of something, for this would remove any guilt on the emperor's part.

Fortunately, some soldiers arrive and save León's life. They threaten the emperor with death should he ever kill León. Instead of being grateful, León considers this to be treason and tells his father that he would still gladly die for him, but now he cannot since the soldiers would then kill the emperor.

Through his unusual interpretation of the father-son relationship, León has fashioned his own quandary. By remaining alive, he presumably poses a threat to the emperor's position because he may wish to claim his rightful crown. By dying, he poses a threat to the emperor's life as well as to the latter's reputation, for León's death would destroy his father's fame.

The emperor's solution is to exile León. When he later writes a letter to his son asking him to return, León does not refuse:

> I owe him . . . honor
> which thus far he has given me;
> I owe him his having engendered me,

> and I owe him much love.
> I must not be cruel to him,
> and I owe him increased honor,
> I owe him existence and life
> and I ought to die for him.

(II, 391)

Accordingly, León acknowledges that anything he owns, including his very existence, is due to his father. Not only does he exist physically because his father engendered him, but his existence in the sense of having honor is the result of his being the son of the emperor.

There follows a series of love intrigues among other characters in the play, culminating in the tying to a tree of Rosaura, who is in love with, and is loved by, León. Under orders from the traitor Mauricio, Rosaura is tied and left alone. General Rosauro, just returned from the battlefield as a conquering hero, finds Rosaura, his sister. What brother and sister have to say to each other under these circumstances is of high importance to this study and therefore, despite its length, I present a free translation of a major portion of their conversation here:

GENERAL: When to the sound of my victory
           fame with greater fury
           goes writing my glory,
           with the stains of this injury
           you try to erase me from history?
           When I take from war
           the fruit of my deeds,
           when my courage terrifies it
           in the strangest lands,
           you affront me in my land?
           . . . .
           with the blood of the one who affronts me
           I want to cancel out the grievance
           . . . .
           for I'm affronting myself
           so long as I don't avenge myself;
           and so that no one may praise it
           I shall kill anyone who knows it,
           for the affront of a serious man
           doesn't die well, if he who causes it

> and he who knows of it doesn't die as well.
> To give death, then, I undertake
> to all those whom I shall see
> who know what I am seeing,
> and I shall go around killing them
> as they go around knowing it;
>
> . . . .

ROSAURA: Kill me.
GENERAL: I promise you
             that I'll give you death,
             but it's got to be in secret,
             so that my affront will also be.

(II, 417)

The general's opening lines show the relationship between honor and fame. As in León's case earlier, it is the personified form, Fame, that is writing the glory and reputation of the general. But this brilliant history is being erased by the injury; in short, he has lost his honor.

Vengeance must be taken immediately; any delay is a further affront, imparted by the general himself. But this vengeance will be taken upon the evidence of the stain on his honor: his sister. It is she, the victim, who by her continued existence reveals the stain. Therefore, only her blood will wash off that stain. Rosaura's laconic answer reveals that she fully concurs: "Kill me."

Moreover, the question of *honra* will arise if knowledge of the affront becomes public. Consequently, anyone who knows of the affront must likewise be killed: the vengeance must be taken in secrecy, since a witness to the vengeance would know of the affront.

It turns out that Rosaura's death is not required for the restoration of honor. Mauricio, frightened by the arrival of the general, confesses his guilt to the emperor, who dispatches soldiers to the scene. The latter arrive in time to save Rosaura's life. León will now marry Rosaura, thus honoring her and her brother. As for Mauricio, it is León's wish that he be only exiled, for it was his confession that enabled the soldiers to save Rosaura's life.

To sum up: the conception of honor and fame is a reaffirmation of concepts found in the dramatists previously studied. The novelty in this work is the relationship of obedience and honor as interpreted by León, who predicates his behavior on what is fundamentally a conventional notion: that one owes obedience to one's emperor and one's father. What is unusual about León's conduct is that he can interpret this commonplace only from an absolute point of view.

CHAPTER 7

Boil

D ON Carlos Boil Vives de Canesma was born in 1577, the illegitimate son of Don Valeriano Boil. He was legitimized,
according to the custom of the time, by an act of the *cortes* of
1585.[1] In 1592 he joined the *Academia de los Nocturnos* under the
pseudonym of *Recelo* ("Distrust").[2] Like his father, Carlos was
involved in many amorous intrigues and met his death as the result
of one of these intrigues on December 8, 1617.[3]

Boil's only drama, *El marido asigurado* (The Reassured Husband), unlike Beneyto's only play, has been the object of praise from
the critics. Mesonero Romanos twice refers to it as a "discreet" (i.e.,
composed with wit) drama and asserts that in his judgment, the play
can stand comparison with the best of our early dramatists.[4]
Mérimée (p. 639) saw great promise in Boil's work, concluding that
the play, sparkling with zest, drawn with firmness, with a portrayal
of characters that stand out and a well-ordered structure of the
episodes, was rich with promise.

In this play, Sigismundo, king of Naples, is about to greet for the
first time his bride Menandra, daughter of the king of Sicily. In
order to assure himself that his new wife will cause him no dishonor,
Sigismundo intends to test her by pretending to be Count Manfredo
who, in turn, will pass himself off as the king.

Readers familiar with the *curioso impertinente* ("the imperti-
nently curious one") episode in *Don Quixote* (or the *comedia*
adaptation by Valencia's Guillén de Castro) will recognize some
common elements between the two plots. The differences, however, are fundamental and far outnumber the similarities.

The difference between the king's scheme in this play and that of
Anselmo in *El curioso impertinente* is manifest: not only does the
husband allow his friend to live with the wife, but he has arranged
matters so that the wife believes that the man with whom she is

living is her husband. Consequently, the matter of love is almost entirely neglected. Sigismundo is not trying to find out whether Menandra loves him since he has allowed her to believe that he is Manfredo. In fact, should she happen to fall in love with him, Sigismundo would not be pleased at all, for this would reveal that Menandra cannot be entrusted with the honor of her husband. This then, and only this, is what Sigismundo wishes to ascertain: regardless of which man Menandra believes to be her husband, will she endanger his honor or will she prove to be a worthy defender of the honor of the king?

Sigismundo's first effort to test Menandra's fidelity consists of arousing her jealousy. Suggesting that her "husband" is having an affair with another woman, Sigismundo urges her to have an affair of her own. However, Menandra is more concerned with her honor than with her jealousy, although she is nonetheless interested in knowing the identity of the other woman. Since this other woman is the invention of Sigismundo, he is at a loss to choose a name. As he explains in an aside, "My doubt shouldn't surprise anyone, for to put someone's honor in doubt is not becoming to an honorable person" (II, 431). In other words, his deception cannot go so far that he involves the honor of an honorable person. Sigismundo explains this once again when he subsequently informs Manfredo of his conversation with Menandra. In answer to Manfredo's question whether Sigismundo had revealed the name of a lady, Sigismundo replies, "No, count; for with a woman even when joking there's got to be respect in dealing with her reputation" (II, 434). The last two quotations, incidentally, show how closely honor and reputation are related and that they are, at times, barely distinguishable.

Manfredo's concern is based on the very real fact that he is in love with Fulgencia, sister of Sigismundo. Since Manfredo has been courting Fulgencia for some time now, such behavior in the palace under the king's nose would constitute an affront to the king, should it become known. Fulgencia makes her feelings on this subject known when she reveals to Manfredo her jealousy as the result of his agreeing to pose as another woman's husband (II, 437). By having allowed Manfredo to make love to her, Fulgencia has, of course, placed the honor of her brother in jeopardy. However, this is so not only because Sigismundo is her brother, but because it is an affront to the king for any woman to engage in a love affair in the palace. Accordingly, when Menandra finds a love letter written to her

"husband" Manfredo, she shows it to Sigismundo in the belief that it
was written by the fictitious woman invented by Sigismundo earlier.
When she tells Sigismundo that there is no doubt that the woman
who wrote the letter lives in the palace, the king's reaction is shock,
and, in a series of asides, he reveals his rage:

> Oh, traitor! May God destroy you;
> oh, enemy of my fame!
> . . . .
> My most intimate friend,
> My most trusted one,
> that one has taken my honor away?
> . . . .
> Oh, honor in the hands of females!
> . . . .
> I shall punish, traitor
> Manfredo, your deceptions.
>
> (II, 444)

Thus the king feels that his honor has been stained by both
Manfredo ("traitor") and Fulgencia ("enemy of my fame"). Yet,
despite his lamentation that honor is in the hands of women, it is
Manfredo whom he intends to punish. Accordingly, Sigismundo
accuses Manfredo of having abused his position as confidant of the
king, since his love affair with Fulgencia is an affront to the king,
"for under the cloak of favor you have dealt in my palace in disregard
of my honor" (II, 446). Sigismundo therefore intends to kill Manfredo. This, he asserts, will put an end to his problem and will put a
stop to public gossip. In other words, he will erase the stain
(Manfredo) on his honor and prevent the erosion of his fame
(reputation) on which that honor depends:

> I'll take away your life,
> so that my worry will end
> by its being ended.
> Let your common blood wash
> these stains through my dagger,
> so that the inhuman mouth
> of your breast and your wound
> close the mouth of the vain masses.
>
> (II, 446)

Manfredo avoids the punishment by telling Sigismundo that he
was only following the latter's orders and that in order to make

Menandra jealous, Manfredo was merely pretending to have an
affair with Fulgencia. As the king is taken in by this ruse, Manfredo
suggests that Menandra be told that Fulgencia is only pretending to
be his sister. Delighted with this scheme, Sigismundo advises
Manfredo to continue with it, suggesting that he make love to
Fulgencia whenever possible in order to arouse Menandra's
jealousy. What dramatic irony there is, then, in the king's comment
as he sees Manfredo making love to Fulgencia: "You are after all as
honorable as you are worthy of my honor; you leave me quite obligated" (II, 453).

As Sigismundo had planned, Menandra's jealousy is aroused. Her
first reaction is to want to commit suicide. As she is about to stab
herself, Sigismundo stops her and the following conversation takes
place:

MENANDRA: Oh, friend!, for this trouble
               which afflicts and torments me
               has an effect so mortal
               that its antidote is . . .
               my death.
SIGISMUNDO: Don't say things like that,
               for your cruelty differs
               from Christian law.
MENANDRA: Note that I'm punishing my wickedness,
               and you'd better let me kill myself
               even for Christianity.
SIGISMUNDO: You're acting like a heretic with your
               afflictions.
MENANDRA: Rather I am a faithful Christian,
               for by giving death to my jealousy
               I exile and kill the Lucifer
               who has conquered my heavens.

                                                 (II, 454)

Here, for the first time in the works analyzed in this study, there is a
desire for death based not on lost honor (although honor is indirectly
involved), but on jealousy. The evil of which Menandra speaks is the
jealousy she feels; its only antidote is death. Refuting Sigismundo's
admonition that suicide is unchristian, Menandra retorts that by
killing herself she will be killing the evil jealousy within her. Far
from being an act of heresy, she views this as a Christian act for she
would be imitating God, who banished and sent to Hell (in a sense,
killed) Lucifer, traditional prototype of jealousy.

However, Sigismundo's suggestion that it would be more appropriate to kill the cause of her jealousy is accepted by Menandra, who decides to kill Fulgencia:

> Note that if she stops living
> it isn't possible to give me death;
> for the kind they can give me—
> justice or severe rigor,
> bearing in mind that
> it is because I killed first—
> is bound to resuscitate me.

(II, 454)

So it is possible that jealousy produces a reaction akin to that which dishonor kindles. For this reason, Menandra believes that if she is punished with death for her murder of Fulgencia, it will not be death in any but the physical sense. Having killed Fulgencia first will be to Menandra what an honor killing may be to someone else. The mention she makes of her resuscitation has its parallel in the other life of the man who dies with honor. Just as the man of honor does not fear death because his fame may live on, so Menandra is not frightened by the thought of her death, for by killing the Devil (jealousy) one does a noble deed: "And although mortals fear death, I didn't fear it . . . for it isn't dying to die for the sake of killing evils" (II, 460).

The relationship of jealousy to honor has been examined by Alpern, who points out that jealousy "is a theme which, being closely related to the *pundonor*, reflects the national temper of the Spaniard."[5] As for the reaction of the person afflicted by jealousy, this "is not only limited to the torture of mind and agony of the heart evidenced by facial manifestations. Blood must be shed. Revenge must be taken, if immediate satisfaction be not offered, or the reparation of a wrong be impossible. . . . Revenge is exercised for the same general reason that we desire restitution when we crave forgiveness on the one hand or exact apology on the other."[6]

Fulgencia is not killed, however, because the true identities of Manfredo and Sigismundo are revealed before matters are allowed to go too far. Manfredo and Fulgencia are given permission to marry by the king, who is delighted by the honorable character of Menandra.

In conclusion, Carlos Boil presents the testing of a woman by her husband in order to learn whether his new bride will be capable of preserving his honor. Menandra's reaction to her jealousy serves as an indication of how well she will protect that honor. The relationship of jealousy to honor is manifested also by the absence of love as an important motif in the Sigismundo-Menandra-Manfredo triangle. Sigismundo is concerned exclusively with the honor which he must entrust to his wife. He never shows any concern for the possibility that Menandra might fall in love with her "husband" Manfredo. Menandra, for her part, becomes jealous over an affair which appears to wreck her marriage, but her realization in the end that her real husband is Sigismundo causes her no regrets.

CHAPTER 8

Turia

RICARDO de Turia is the pseudonym under which the Valencian magistrate Don Pedro Juan de Rejaule y Toledo wrote his literary works. Although Turia's identity as Rejaule was rejected by Mesonero Romanos[1] and although Juliá accepts it only tentatively, Mérimée does believe him to have been the magistrate, and Martí Grajales quotes Onofre Izquierdo to show that poet and magistrate were one and the same. "As is seen," concludes Martí Grajales, "the affirmation is categorical and leaves no room for doubt."[2]

Turia was born in Valencia and was baptized on August 3, 1578. He studied law and by September 13, 1600, the date of his marriage, held the doctorate. The date of his death is unknown.

Both Juliá and Mérimée note a lack of originality in Turia's works. Juliá concludes that Turia is a disciple of Tárrega, Aguilar, and Guillén de Castro (p. cxvii). Mérimée observes that the plays evoke developments already known and that Turia is a docile pupil of superior masters (p. 641).

I La Belligera Española

A cursory glance at the cast of characters of *La belligera española* (The Belligerent Spanish Lady) reveals that this play was inspired by Ercilla's epic poem *La Araucana*. As the first act opens, Lautaro and Rauco, two Araucanian Indians, quarrel over a letter which Rauco is carrying. At this point in the plot it is not yet clear whether it is a letter from the valiant Rengo to Guacolda, Lautaro's betrothed, or whether Guacolda had sent the letter to Rengo. In either case, Lautaro considers it an offense and takes the letter from Rauco, who warns Lautaro that he is risking the wrath of Rengo, a man to be feared. Lautaro replies that he would already have killed Rauco, were it not precisely for Rengo's valor. His reason is not fear, however, for he explains that Rauco is not worth killing,

110

> for if that man [Rengo] weren't
> so unique in courage,
> with whose life I must give
> life and vengeance to my name,
> of your vile procurings
> you'd see, infamous one, the reward,
> for my fire would already have undone
> you into cold ashes,
> and my sighs would toss you
> to the wind which undoes them,
> because of a man who does such a thing,
> even ashes wouldn't remain.
>
> (II, 518–19)

Since Rengo is a man of valor, his death at the hands of Lautaro would provide the latter with revenge and give life to Lautaro's name. In a word, it would give Lautaro fame. On the other hand, the death of the go-between Rauco would not bestow fame, since his vile behavior renders him infamous. Death for such a man would be equivalent to complete annihilation, such as befell the husband in Artieda's *The Lovers*. In the meantime, Rengo's men had abducted Guacolda, and now Lautaro promptly rescues her. Rather than thank him, Guacolda tells Lautaro:

> I don't want, husband and lord,
> words of mine to render today
> thanks to your courage,
> for you watched for your own honor
> if you were fighting for me.
>
> (II, 522)

Since Guacolda is Lautaro's betrothed, what happens to her affects his honor. Therefore, by rescuing her, Lautaro was really rescuing himself, since his existence depends metaphorically upon his honor. Moreover, since Guacolda is still unmarried, her fate also determines the honor of her father. The latter is therefore grateful to Lautaro for having protected his honor: what is more, the father, in view of his advanced age, now comes to realize that his honor is in Lautaro's hands (II, 523).

There follows a resurgence of the war between the Spaniards and the Araucanians. Lautaro, who had first sided with the Spaniards in the hope of punishing Rengo, is dismayed by the lack of valor of his countrymen:

> is it possible that death frightens you,
> and servitude doesn't have you scared?
> How is it that death, when it is honorable,
> is not sweeter and more savory than slavery?
>
> (II, 529)[3]

Consequently, having convinced his compatriots that death is preferable to slavery, Lautaro leads them into battle against the Spaniards, with the result that the Spanish general, Valdivia, is killed by Lautaro. Valdivia's final words are a series of curses upon Lautaro:

> May you not attain your full age,
> and in the middle of the course
> of that commenced luck, let
> it take from you, ingrate, your life.
> Die if you are captured
> in front of your lady, unjust one,
> not because you'll go happily that way,
> but so that you can regret more
> the loss of your life and pleasure.
> To the one who attempts your death
> may your widow get married.
>
> (II, 530)

In the meantime, Guacolda had left her home and is now near the battlefield, hoping to be together with Lautaro. It is at this point that we finally learn that the letter which caused the struggle at the beginning of the play had not been written by Guacolda but by another Indian girl who was in love with Ranco. The act of this girl, says Guacolda, "risked my life, or my honor, beloved possession, for there is no life without honor" (II, 532). For Guacolda, as for so many other men and women in the Golden Age *comedia,* honor is equivalent to life.

Lautaro, having been informed of Guacolda's whereabouts, now comes in search of his beloved, but fails to find her. Momentarily torn between his duty to return to the battlefield and his desire to rescue her, Lautaro decides that he must do his duty as a soldier, considering his personal desires ("pleasure and love") subordinate to his honor even if it means the possibility of Guacolda's being dead, for "the more takes away from the less" (II, 535).

The success of the Indians on the battlefield has now caused the Spaniards to lose heart, which dismays Doña Mencía, who determines to arouse her countrymen:

> The strongest heart is
> pressured by fear;
> but the consideration
> of one's fame and reputation
> necessarily must have its effect.
> Let's go forth and meet them,
> for if God favors me
> today they'll restore their honor.
>
> (II, 540)

Accordingly, although even the stoutest heart may be subject to fear, one's fame must have greater weight. Since Mencía is referring to the people who are now on their way out of the city, she apparently feels that this act of cowardice has already deprived them of their honor; therefore she talks of the restoration of that honor which, as is seen from the fourth line, is linked to one's fame and reputation. Her success in turning the tide is evidenced by the praise which Rengo showers upon her:

> You who with your great deeds
> resuscitate the memory,
> in order to give it new death,
> of the strong Amazons,
> for we recall them
> through your famous deeds,
> and we forget them
> through your heroic feats.
>
> (II, 545)

This is an interesting passage. Mencía's deeds recall the heroic feats of the legendary Amazons, only to obliterate them by virtue of her own feats, which are of greater glory.

II   La Fe Pagada

Turia's *La fe pagada* (Faith Repaid) is the final work to be analyzed in this study of the Valencian dramatists. As this play opens, Prince Leonardo welcomes Captain Ludovico back from the battlefield. The prince is in love with Teodora, Ludovico's cousin, but she has rejected him for the past three years. Ludovico, on the other hand, has come to court his cousin, having fallen in love with her picture. Ludovico's official reason for his presence, however, is that his uncle Conrado (Teodora's father) had asked him to watch over Teodora and her mother Claudia, during Conrado's absence in Naples. In other words, Conrado has come to realize the dangers involved in leaving the two women in his life without the protection of a male relative. These fears have also been the source of anguish for Claudia, who tells Teodora:

My husband and your sire / attends so phlegmatically to matters of his honor? / A wife and a daughter are to be left alone / and without protection in sight of the enemy? (II, 615)

Claudia is concerned not so much with her own safety as with her husband's honor, so she is well aware that it is upon her fate that Conrado's honor depends. Accordingly, when war breaks out, Claudia decides that she and Teodora would do well to flee. Ludovico shares this feeling and flees with the two women, causing Leonardo to become so angry that he bites the messenger who brings him this news.

Ludovico and Teodora manage to escape to Moorish territory, where they are attacked by a band of men. Teodora hides in a cave while Ludovico fights the Moors, who defeat him and leave him for dead. When Teodora escapes through another opening in the cave, she sees the Moorish ships sailing off and, in the belief that Ludovico had been taken aboard, she hails the ships and begs them to return for her. The ships do return, and one of the Moors remarks how strange it is to see a woman request to be taken prisoner.

In the meantime, Conrado has heard of the war and finally remembers his responsibilities, but the recognition of his failure to protect his honor is too late, for Leonardo had defeated the Moorish boats, rescued Teodora, and now, as Conrado comes upon them, Leonardo is attempting to rape Teodora. Drawing his sword, Conrado explains to the surprised Leonardo that it is necessary "to wash with your treacherous blood the stain of my dishonor" (II, 638). It is noteworthy that Conrado is not raising his sword against his prince in order to protect his daughter against further injury (she has not yet been raped), but exclusively in order to wipe out his own dishonor. Despite the fact that Teodora has not yet been deprived of her virginity, the dishonor is a *fait accompli*. Moreover, Conrado gives no thought to the killing of his daughter other than to remove the evidence of the dishonor; he is motivated only by a desire to restore his honor.[4]

Conrado is unable to pursue his desire, however, for the prince's soldiers intervene. Conrado now asks for death rather than imprisonment, because not only does imprisonment mean loss of liberty, but such a life, without honor (since he was not able to restore his honor through vengeance), is intolerable. Leonardo, on the other hand, has a different fate in store for them, preferring to force Conrado to witness the rape of his daughter. This kind of dishonor would be even more serious than the one already administered, because Conrado would be unable to demonstrate his *hombría*. That is to say, Conrado would be without honor not only because someone did something to him or to his daughter, but because Conrado himself failed to prevent or avenge the dishonor.

We are not informed of what happens next until some time later in the play when Conrado appears, meets Claudia, and relates to his wife the events just described: "The process of my own dishonor I went to see" (II, 648), he laments, adding that a storm destroyed the ship on which he, Teodora, and Leonardo were traveling. Conrado managed to get to shore on a wooden board, but he does not know the fate of Teodora. Claudia is upset at the thought of the danger in which Conrado left their daughter (thinking of the shipwreck), but Conrado points out that a greater danger lies in the fact that he was forced to leave Teodora at the mercy of Leonardo, for this further endangers Conrado's honor. He thus considers the possibility of Teodora's death as subordinate to the dangers inherent in his inability to protect her from Leonardo.

Leonardo and Teodora had also managed to escape with their lives and now, once again, Leonardo tries to rape Teodora. This time, they happen to be within sight of the prison in which Ludovico is held captive. We now learn that Teodora considers Ludovico her husband (evidently the *palabra de esposo*, "promise to wed," had been given at some time prior to these events). Consequently, Ludovico's honor is involved. Leonardo finds this to be exactly what he wanted, for now he can force Ludovico to witness his own dishonor, just as he had hoped to do with Conrado. Once more, however, Leonardo is prevented from carrying out his intentions, for Rosana and some Moors arrive in time to save Teodora. (Rosana later turns out to be the long-lost sister of Teodora, but at the moment she is thought to be a Moorish woman.) Teodora's virginity is left intact, thus saving her reputation. As for Ludovico himself, he has been spared the dishonor of becoming a cuckold, "for you have avenged my horns" (II, 651).

All the principal characters of the play now come together, Conrado still preferring death to the intolerable life without honor that he feels he is leading. However, all the problems of honor are now resolved in a flash as Rosana's identity is disclosed. Leonardo will marry Rosana and Ludovico will marry Teodora. Consequently, as is customary in the *comedia,* marriage restores order and with it honor.

III   *Turia: The Conventional* Comedia

I must agree with the observations of Mérimée and Juliá cited at the beginning of this chapter with respect to the lack of originality in Turia's plays. It should come as no surprise, then, that in regard to the matters analyzed in this study as a whole, I can say that in the plays of Turia I find confirmation of the concepts discovered in the previous dramatists.

A letter from or to one's betrothed can be considered an affront (if the receiver or the sender is someone other than the fiancé). The vengeance of such an affront serves no purpose if it is administered to a person who is considered to be without honor. Moreover, death for the latter would be equivalent to annihilation, since the lack of honor precludes any fame as a basis for that "other life."

In *Faith Repaid,* it is demonstrated that a man's honor depends on the fate of the women for whom he is responsible, for if he cannot protect them or avenge any wrong done to them, he has failed to display his *hombría,* which, as we have seen on repeated occasions, is one of the bases of honor. Since dishonor is figuratively equivalent to death, a man who cannot recover his honor prefers physical death to a life of shame. However, it is not always necessary to restore honor through bloodshed; this may also be accomplished through matrimony, in view of the order and harmony symbolized by marriage. Death, we saw, may be considered as more attractive than slavery or, at the very least, a pleasant form of bondage. Death may be preferable to an unwanted marriage, but if the death of a loved one may be avenged by means of such a marriage, then the marriage becomes preferable to death.

The findings listed above, none of which reveals a novel approach to the matters under analysis, reflect the lack of originality of the dramatic art of Ricardo de Turia.

CHAPTER 9

A Perspective for the Valencian Drama

I The Two Sides of the Coin

IN chapter 2, I translated at length from the verses of Jorge Manrique which are so essential for a comprehension of the works analyzed in this book, as well as for that of the *comedia* in general and for much of Spanish literature of the Golden Age as a whole. I did not, of course, mean to imply that Manrique appeared spontaneously with a developed set of ideas about such an involved concept, any more than I can accept the proposition that Lope de Vega in one day (or even in one lifetime) "created" the *comedia*. But Jorge Manrique occupies a proper place at the beginning of this book, for, while he, too, belongs in a lengthy evolutionary process, it was the set of ideas as he presented them that was to become the Foundation for the *comedias* of the Valencians and for the national *comedia* of Lope and his followers.

I use the term "foundation" with deliberate care, particularly in view of Reichenberger's thesis, cited in chapter 1, that the *comedia* rests on the two rocks of faith and honor. Manrique's verses take in both concepts and represent the apparent dichotomy between the three theological virtues of faith, hope, and charity and the four worldly virtues of prudence, justice, temperance, and fortitude. The *comedias* analyzed in this book clearly depend more heavily for their dramatic content on the second group, the so-called worldly or natural virtues. Although the discussion of the nature of virtue can be traced back even earlier, for example, to Plato and Aristotle, I believe that Cicero was the first to identify the problem as it would, centuries later, become a central point of the Spanish *comedia:* "Since all moral rectitude springs from four sources (one of which is prudence; the second, social instinct; the third, courage; the fourth, temperance), it is often necessary in deciding a question of duty that these virtues be weighed against one another."[1]

118

What, then, is honor? A concise description is provided by Watson: "Honor as a man's most precious possession, honor as the testimony of the good opinion of others, and dishonor as a thing to be feared worse than death itself, are notions which are so all-pervasive in the 16th century that we hardly think of them as integral parts of a systematic philosophy. They do, however, mostly stem from Aristotelian definitions of honor in Renaissance textbooks on moral philosophy."[2] Aristotle, then, defines honor as the public recognition of one's worth. Cicero defines the nature of that worth, moral rectitude, as stemming from prudent, social, courageous and temperate behavior. Honor, as a result, cannot exist without its foundation in such virtuous behavior; conversely, virtuous behavior carries with it the basis of honor. As Watson observes, "virtue is as inextricably connected with honor as the body is with its shadow" (p. 3 n.). Consequently, whether we speak of an "inner" honor as synonymous with morally virtuous behavior or of an "outer" honor as the public recognition of one's worthiness, honor and virtue remain two sides of the same coin.

What, then, we must also ask, is virtue? The etymology begins with the Latin *vir* ("man"), whence *virtus*, originally meaning "of (male) strength" and "it soon comes to mean both 'courage' and 'moral worth' (in women, narrowed to 'chastity')."[3] So virtue, like honor, has an inner, moral aspect as well as a recognizable behavior, a duality which clarifies Cicero's linking of moral rectitude with worldly attributes like courage and social instinct.

In chapter 3, I cited Atkinson's judgment that Virués is the link between Seneca and Lope. Seneca, whom the Spaniards often claim as a Spaniard because of his birth in what is now Cordova,[4] is generally grouped with the Stoics (an oversimplification of a diverse philosophical group of thinkers, in my opinion) and is therefore considered to be in opposition to the concepts I have been describing. Yet, a perceptive study by Neal Wood sheds light on Seneca's understanding of virtue and other matters pertinent to my study of the development of the themes and motifs of the Valencian precursors of Lope de Vega.

Wood acknowledges that Seneca's perception of virtue has as its essential notion the idea of moral goodness. Nonetheless, he finds that "central to the outlook of Seneca is a conception of the eternal struggle between *virtus* and *fortuna*. Although the idea is common in classical thought . . . Seneca's continual emphasis on and extensive discussion of the contest and the way he describes it are without parallel. On all the major points he makes . . . , Seneca feels compelled to resort to military language and metaphor. When discussing *virtus*, he refers to the moral journey of man through life. Nevertheless, he realizes that *virtus* is a quality *most characteristically displayed under battlefield conditions* [italics mine]. . . ."[5] Wood also refers to Seneca's essay to Lucilius on Providence in which Seneca remarks that "the brave stoic soldier will rejoice with each attack of fortune because he realizes that adversity and hardship are the test of his *manliness and virtue* [italics mine again]."[6]

In an epistle on crowds, Seneca advises Lucilius to "scorn the satisfaction which comes from popular approval. The many admire you, but have you grounds for self-satisfaction? . . ."[7] This would seem to suggest that Seneca has no use for reputation or external recognition, and to a large extent this is so. Yet, his writings are sprinkled with utterances such as "I account you unfortunate because you have never been unfortunate. You have passed through life without an adversary; no one can know your potentiality, not even you."[8] Such statements bring us back on the path of seeing virtue in Cicero's terms, namely, that without courage, fortitude, social awareness, etc., virtue is not realized. Seneca comes close to equating virtue with self-esteem as the result of virile acts in response to adversities. If Seneca is to be included among the Stoics, then, I cannot agree with Watson's unqualified distinction that "the opinion of others is not to be ignored [in the Renaissance] as in the ancient Stoic or medieval Christian scheme, but is to give satisfaction by confirming one's inner sense of honor" (pp. 94–95). Seneca does indeed give far greater importance to one's inner sense of honor, but, as his words above indicate, he shares in the need to have that inner sense confirmed. Moreover, Seneca's conclusion that "death hallows men whose mode of dying is praised even by those who dread it,"[9] while it concentrates on the mode of dying rather than of living, when added to his previously cited observation on passing through life (and to Wood's views on Seneca's understanding of *virtus* as related to virility), gives increased weight to my belief that Seneca recognized the relationship among the concepts of moral worth, virile behavior, and public acknowledgement. In short, Seneca belongs, with Aristotle and Cicero, among the classical moralists whose thinking eventually led to Jorge Manrique, the Valencian dramatists, Lope de Vega, and many others (including Cervantes) beyond the scope of this book.

The importance of Manrique has already been suggested, but it takes on increased significance when placed in the context of these last pages. Watson observes that "as Cicero says of Scipio, the exalted hero will be held in perpetual esteem by all posterity and his glory and reputation will never die. Cicero thus achieves permanence for his values; . . . he depends on succeeding generations of men to perpetuate the fame of the great men of the past" (p. 27). Cicero, therefore, transcends death through fame. Glory and reputation, which result from virtuous deeds (as defined by Cicero, equivalent to the worldly virtues), are the means to achieve a dichotomy between death and "never dying."

By the time of the Renaissance, writes Watson, "immortality . . . meant two things—Christian immortality and immortality through posthumous fame" (p. 69). The second half of the dichotomy has been subdivided but the essential element—their relative values—is still missing, despite Watson's quotation from a work as late as 1585, George Whetstone's *A Mirror of Treue Honnour,* in which it is clearly explained that the chief cause of the importance of posthumous fame was "that the auncestors noble monuments might be precedents of honour to their posterities: and, therefore, it was not unproperly said, that the histories of the time were a *second life,* and tooke away a great part of our fears to die" (cited by Watson, p. 143; italics mine).

Américo Castro, in a book significantly titled *Hacia Cervantes* (Toward Cervantes), has commented on Manrique's poem by observing that death has become life and that, of Jorge Manrique's dead father, "more is what we have left than what disappears; the final impression is glorious and affirmative."[10] Orduna, citing Salinas' great study of Jorge Manrique, agrees that death is the major motif of the poem but finds it necessary to add a nuance which is made evident by the structure, at which point he cites Américo Castro's words above.[11]

Orduna is correct, but I am inclined to use a word more emphatic than "nuance" to describe the significance of Castro's observation. Although Castro certainly was not the first to notice it (strictly speaking, it was Jorge Manrique himself, who did not resort to subtleties on this point), the importance of the "nuance" is the interjection of a *second life,* hierarchically speaking, of intermediate length and value between the mortal and immortal varieties of life. The key word in Castro's sentence is "more," just as the key words in Manrique's poem had been the comparative forms "longer" and "better." Consequently, there is no dichotomy between life and death; there is no longer a dichotomy between dying and never dying; there is no need for a debate between Christian immortality and immortality through posthumous fame. Jorge Manrique has enumerated the hierarchical values of *three* levels of life: the physical, of least importance; the life of fame, of greater importance and duration; the eternal, of highest value and imperishable.

I have twice referred to Reichenberger's thesis that the *comedia* rests upon two rocks (or pillars, as he has called them more recently) of honor and faith. Green similarly concludes that the *comedia* is to be thought of "as a collective enterprise built and resting upon the two great collective ideals of the Spaniards: in the secular sphere, *honor;* in the religious, *faith*, the Catholic faith."[12] I believe that a case could be made to show that the religious *comedia* depends upon the theological virtues of faith, hope, and charity, whereas the secular *comedia* draws its inspiration from the worldly virtues of prudence, justice, temperance, and fortitude.

I do not wish to set up a new dichotomy, for the concepts frequently overlap. I am suggesting, however, that much of the Spanish *comedia* is better understood if we relate the religious drama to the theological virtues which lead to the third, eternal life of the soul with God, on the one hand; and on the other, if we understand that the so-called *comedias de honor* are the special contribution of Spanish culture to a code of ethics which has its roots in Aristotle's definition of honor, in Cicero's definition of virtue as the result of living according to the four worldly virtues—among which is fortitude, key to Seneca's understanding of virtue as virile response to adversity—and, finally, in the belief in a second life of glory and fame as the result of virtuous (i.e., virile) defense of one's honor.

Honor and virtue are not, as I have already suggested, placed in opposition. In chapter 1, I referred to Lope de Vega's oft-quoted advice from his *New Art* that honor problems are best because they move everyone forcefully. Much has been made of these words, ranging from the fact that honor is the most important motif to the fact that everyone is moved by it. Relatively little is said of the following words, significantly linked by the conjunction "with." The original Spanish is:

> Los casos de la honra son mejores
> porque mueven con fuerza a toda gente,

> *con ellos las acciones virtuosas,*
> *que la virtud es dondequiera amada*

(vv. 327–30),

which in English means:

> Honor cases are best
> because they move everyone forcefully,
> *with them* virtuous actions,
> for virtue is loved everywhere. (italics mine)

Not only have matters of honor and virtue been joined as my italics imply, but attention has been focused on virtuous *actions*, that is to say, that once more virtue is seen in its Senecan sense of virility or the worldly virtue of fortitude.

Additional light is shed, therefore, on Shervill's observation that "Lope's secular heroines of Spanish ancestry are essentially idealized beings whose virtue, honor and fortitude remain unshaken in the face of temptation or adversity."[13]

II *Virtue and the Virile Valencians*

Early in the chapter on Artieda, I cited not only Artieda himself with respect to his own view as one who saw the need for a new style, but Ebersole's observation that the new drama would deal not with deities or fabulous creatures, but rather with men and women. The imagery continues to make allusions to swans, pelicans, tigers, crocodiles, and even dragons, but the protagonists are now ordinary humans. This is in perfect accord with their yearning for the "second" life of fame and honor, which, as I have tried to show, depends on the four worldly or natural virtues or, as they are often more explicitly called in Spanish, the virtues *del hombre*, "of man." It comes as no surprise, then, that so much weight is given throughout the dramas to the concept of *hombría*.

The very first drama to be discussed rests on the concept of manliness and fortitude as the means for achieving that second and better life of fame. No wonder, then, that in *The Lovers* and subsequent works, the death of a youth, especially when it has not occurred in battle, is viewed so pessimistically, since the individual has had so little time to demonstrate his manliness. (Significantly, the quality of innocence is not a factor in achieving the life of honor.)

Much has been made of the difference between Virués' *Elisa*

Dido and his other plays. It would be tempting, therefore, to dismiss *Elisa Dido* as an attempt to imitate another age and consider only the four plays which Virués himself distinguished as the kind being used in the theater of his day, particularly when at first blush, so much is made of the characters' loss of at least two of the theological virtues, faith and hope. It would also be easy to ignore this play as an anachronism if theological virtues are to be mixed with pagan times. Yet, just as Lope, Calderón, and others were to adapt classical figures to Spanish conventions, so here Virués has combined pagan fate and Christian providence and challenged what Hermenegildo calls "the heroine's virile energy."[14] Dido, therefore, is one of the first virile women in the Spanish theater, a woman who views the world as a "bitter war," a woman who speaks of her death as "a great victory," in short, a woman endowed with fortitude and, as Sargent has observed, with prudence.

Virility is so patently evident in Semíramis that I need not restate my words in chapter 3 other than to add that what upon first reading may have seemed a monstrosity now assumes thematic significance within the present context. Atila similarly represents an exaggerated version of virility, but his honor is not the two-sided coin of fame *and* moral rectitude any more than is that of Semíramis. For this reason, neither of these protagonists achieves that life of honor. Acts intended for external recognition which are not balanced by the Aristotelian and Ciceronian definitions of virtue lead to no honor and hence to no reward, be it temporal or long-lasting.

Accordingly, Virués felt it necessary, in the prologue to *Cruel Casandra*, to define virtue (see note 46 to chapter 3). In addition to the previously analyzed words concerning the relative merits of virtue and blood, this prologue reinforces the necessity of beginning virtuous behavior early in life ("virtue is advisable in the youth") and the honor-bestowing comfort which a life of virtue provides for the aged ("in the old it is honorable and delightful"). In any event, whether Virués is presenting examples to be followed or avoided, the virile woman, often dressed in male attire, is a characteristic of his theater. As Hermenegildo has pointed out, "the fact is that we are in the presence of an ambiguity that plays with the man-woman or woman-man theme. This doubt is explained within the totality of the entire work of Virués. And what cannot be questioned is the fact that it is a matter of a woman who conducts herself in the life of the court by means of a masculine appearance."[15]

III   *The Valencian "School"*

As Hermenegildo attempts to define Virués' place in the development of Spain's national theater, he suggests that what he calls "the Valencian movement" was headed by Virués and that "the new Valencian taste received its impulse from Virués." He goes on to differentiate Virués from Artieda, partly because of the former's specific taste for horror as well as because the general artistic temperaments of both artists oppose each other.[16] I cannot disagree with Hermenegildo with respect to his generalities about the two Valencian dramatists, but I must ask where words such as "headed" (*encabezado*), "impulse," and "movement" find their significance.

Clearly we have arrived at a crucial point of definition, namely, that of the existence of a Valencian "school" of drama. I addressed this problem early in this work, avoiding the conclusion temporarily by presenting well-known scholars' views on both sides of the question pending an examination of the works themselves. I should evade the issue no longer. Let me begin with two definitions, the first from a dictionary:

[A school is a] body of persons that are or have been taught by a particular master . . . ; hence, a body or succession of persons who are disciples of the same master, or who are united by a general similarity of principles and methods 1612; also, a type or brand of doctrine or practice 1892. b. *fig.* A set of persons who agree in certain opinions, etc. 1798.[17]

The second quotation, although specifically aimed at one discipline, has certain general truths:

Leaving aside the question of the merits of schools, it is obvious that there can only be schools—i.e., differing views and allegiances—where crucial issues are still unsettled. We do not find two or more schools of thought regarding a problem where one answer has been accepted.[18]

Undoubtedly, an endless number of definitions could be paraded here, but the two cited above contain the basic ingredients, of which three stand out: (1) there must be some communality of beliefs, methods, or approach; (2) there must exist at least one other group of comparable importance whose views on crucial matters differ substantially; (3) a school must have a leader.

I cannot share Hermenegildo's view that Virués headed what he

calls the Valencian movement. Not only does this oppose Juliá's
opinion that Virués was not in the mainstream, but I have difficulty
thinking of which authors Virués led. To say that his work led to
Lope is one thing; to say that he led an entire movement is quite
another, and no substantiation for such a position for Virués exists.[19]
Froldi finds Tárrega to be the most important of the Valencian
dramatists under discussion; not only does Froldi himself reject the
notion of a school, however, but I would have to add that being the
most important member of a literary group (in the sense that his
productions are the most noteworthy) does not necessarily imply the
exercise of leadership, much less the presence of a school. With
regard to the other two criteria, I pointed out in chapter 1 that what
all these poets had in common was their interest in composing
comedias, but other groups in other places, notably Seville, were
doing similar things and so the criterion of other schools of thought
does not provide any evidence that a "school" of drama existed in
Valencia (although many individuals criticized the *comedia* in
general and Lope in particular during the apogee of the genre's
popularity).

It is interesting to note, as I briefly indicated in chapter 1, that
while there are some who insist on the existence of a school, there
are others who barely acknowledge that any Valencian dramatists
existed and still others who deny that anything called *comedia* can
be said to exist without Lope de Vega. Let me deal with the last
group quickly and then attempt to put the Valencians in their
proper perspective.

Although it was written more than half a century ago, Rennert's
The Spanish Stage in the Time of Lope de Vega concluded that "the
importance of Valencia as a theatrical center has generally been
exaggerated," adding that "there is no evidence of any unusual
dramatic activity in Valencia before the arrival of Lope de Vega in
that city in 1588" (p. 191). Rennert then goes on to make the in-
credible judgment that "it is to Lope's sojourn in Valencia in 1588–
90 that the powerful impulse which the drama received in that city
is wholly due. He was the founder of the Valencian School, for we
hear nothing of it before Lope visited Valencia, and that the latter
city was always dependent upon Madrid in theatrical matters is
shown by abundant evidence" (p. 192). I trust that the preceding
chapters of this book, added to the work of scholars like Mérimée,

Juliá, and Froldi, reveal the folly of Rennert's sweeping general-izations.[20]

I have already referred to Rennert's colleague, Américo Castro, and his insistence that the *comedia* was "created" by Lope, although his words (see chapter 1) at least suggest that Lope had antecedents. This opinion is shared by López Morales, whose only reference to any Valencian is the previously cited footnote on why Lope chose to name Virués rather than Cueva in his *El laurel de Apolo;* by Margaret Wilson, who makes one brief reference to Virués and one to Turia and concludes that her subject "is the *comedia* created by Lope."[21] Finally, an outstanding scholar like Otis Green finds it possible to speak of Lope's *comedia* by repeating, "I say *his*, because it was he and not his brilliant predecessor Torres Naharro who imposed this typical form on the Spanish nation."[22] Aside from my surprise that Green concludes that any individual "imposed" such a major form on an entire nation, I do not understand how Green accounts for the better than threescore years between Torres Naharro and Lope de Vega. Did nothing happen?

I have previously cited the review of Froldi's first edition by Fucilla, who asked the question, "Has Mr. Froldi . . . succeeded in vanquishing the myths that have prevailed about Lope and the creation of the comedia?" The above comments would indicate that myths are difficult to destroy. More presumptuous, however, is the review by Morby who asks, "Why, meanwhile [in the absence of 'extremely precise' dates for individual plays], is it necessary to submit a case at all? . . ."[23] The works of Artieda, Virués, Tárrega, and Aguilar should supply the answer to this question, which by its very nature questions the value of literary investigation. What is more, I fail to understand the need to modify the word "precise" by the adverb "extremely." Dates are either precise or imprecise. The stipulation becomes ironic when Morby himself writes that "one must perforce believe that [Lope] had begun to write [*comedias*] in preadolescence; which, being true (and in the absence of a de-pendable chronology), one must also conclude that he had scores behind him before setting foot in Valencia. His leadership was thus inescapable." How "one" achieves this belief and reaches this conclusion *in the absence of a dependable chronology* while de-manding "extremely precise" dates of another is unanswered.

The proper position of the Valencian dramatists is, as I have been suggesting throughout this book, that of a place in the *evolution* of a genre which reached its zenith with Lope de Vega but which received many of its ingredients at the hands of the Valencians.[24]

IV *The* Comedia *in Valencia*

My apparent digression in the previous section has cleared the way for a picture of what did go on in Valencia, given the fact that Artieda and Virués must be seen as one set of steps and Tárrega and Aguilar as another. Nearly every author mentioned in this book has some champion prepared to name him leader of the Valencians, whether it be Artieda, Virués, Guillén de Castro, or Lope de Vega himself. Tárrega also has some adherents, including the Golden Age moralist Baltasar Gracián, who maintained that "Canon Tárrega seasoned the verses even more and has some very tasty inventions," adding that then "Lope de Vega followed, with his fertility and abundance." Lázaro Carreter, who cites this passage, complains that despite this order of events, so clearly pointed out by Gracián, the critics have refused to accept this judgment, persisting in displaying Lope as a creator on whom everything depends. And the fact is, adds Lázaro, that Tárrega has many Lopean traits to offer,[25] an opinion shared by Martí Grajales, Juliá, Valbuena Prat, and, of course, Froldi, as I indicated in chapter 4.

One of the major characteristics of the Spanish national *comedia* has been clearly identified by Reichenberger in his previously cited "The Uniqueness of the *Comedia*." I am referring to the concept that the typical *comedia* begins with the disruption of the order of things (if not immediately, then very soon after the orderly nature has been presented) and ends with the reestablishment of order, the harmony being reflected most often by matrimony and the restoration of broken honor, the plot serving to demonstrate the fragility of such matters in the world by the difficulty of the characters' attempts to avoid dishonor (real or perceived) and their struggle to recover their honor and hence the renewed order of the microcosmic world each individual represents.

I would have to repeat chapter 4 if I felt it necessary to demonstrate how typical such a pattern is of Tárrega's *comedias*. The same may be said of chapter 5 and the *comedias* of Aguilar. Here, then, is the contribution of the Valencians to the formation of the Spanish national drama: the gradual codification of the basic ingredients, ranging from characters (including the antecedent of the *gracioso*) to themes (which A. A. Parker stresses as the aspect to which even the action itself must be subordinate) and the manner in which these themes may be presented.

The most important theme in the *comedias* discussed here is honor. The most important manner in which to deal with it is fortitude. In this sense, the Valencian *comedia* stands apart—and to a lesser degree, so does the *comedia* of Lope (but, I believe, even less the *comedias* of Tirso and Calderón)—from one aspect which Tillyard has called "the common property of western Europe in the sixteenth century,"[26] namely, the concept of the great chain of being. That the Spaniards shared this concept is evident in nearly all of the literature of the time, much of which is explained in Américo Castro's fundamental *El pensamiento de Cervantes* and without which Reichenberger's observation would not have been possible, nor would much of A. A. Parker's, which relies heavily on poetic justice. The relationship of these ideas to order and the great chain of being is, I trust, obvious.[27]

The one aspect I hinted at above, however, deals with a comment by Tillyard concerning the belief that within each class there was a primate. As one of several examples, he gives justice as having primacy among the virtues (p. 30). I believe that Parker's thesis (and to a great extent, Reichenberger's) is correct for the drama of the *seventeenth* century, since the essential theme of justice (symbolized by order) makes all the action subservient to it. In this way the final scenes of Lope's *Fuente Ovejuna,* Tirso's *El burlador de Sevilla* (the famous *Don Juan* play), and Calderón's *La devoción de la cruz* (Devotion to the Cross) are logically explained. But if my reading of the Valencians is correct, their theme is honor *as* honor and only secondarily honor as a reflection of justice. This is not to say that in the background there did not exist that fundamental understanding of order and the chain of being of which Tillyard speaks. What I am saying is that of the virtues, fortitude, not justice, had primacy in the Valencian *comedias* and this explains why so very frequently it is the *struggle,* the need to exhibit *strength,* that forms the central point of the *comedias*. An excellent example is Tárrega's *The Meadow of Valencia.* If all that were needed to restore order and justice were the matrimony which symbolizes these matters, the play could have ended with the appearance of the couple's uncle, who had urged an immediate wedding. Yet the play continues because the essence of its drama is Laura's continual need to fight the deceptions of society without losing honor.

The other side of the coin is epitomized in Tárrega's *The Constant Duchess,* in which Torcato had attempted to destroy the bonds of matrimony between Flaminia and the duke, commenting that "Heaven is all peace and a disdain is odious war." Not only has Torcato inverted the moral values, but his metaphors of peace and war are inverse descriptions of a woman's honor: it is precisely in the fortitude of woman's behavior as she considers the preservation of honor the only kind of just war that the play finds its meaning and its title.

There are numerous examples of virile behavior in men and women in the *comedias* studied in this book. Another aspect of fortitude resides in the frequent desire for vengeance, since revenge as an action serves to stress one's resolution and strength. This was why, for example, I found it necessary to disagree with Mérimée's interpretation and translation of Aguilar's *Honorable Vengeance,* since more emphasis is placed on the manner (i.e., the honorable, virtuous, and virile way) in which the vengeance was sought. The need for vengeance is intimately related to the need to display virility and in this fashion demonstrates the virtue of fortitude.

Vengeance is so closely tied to the honor concept that it, too, is considered more important than justice. Aguilar's *Hopeless Luck* not only achieves the highly important synthesis of Christian and pagan ethics as I noted in chapter 5—an achievement worth repeating in a concluding chapter—but has Ferdinand the Catholic agree to the concept that justice only punishes and does not satisfy the need for vengeance, that is, although the obligation may have been satisfied, the individual's need to demonstrate his own fortitude remains. I have already quoted La Du to the effect that, while the intervention of the king may indeed be sufficient to restore lost honor in the dramas of Calderón, it is not so in the plays of Valencia's Guillén de Castro. Aguilar, as I have just shown, shares Castro's view, as does Tárrega in *Loyal Blood,* in which even the king must in an aside, confess how he admires the noble breast of Fruela who had killed the offender of the family honor. Doña Lambra as well comments on the honorability of the vengeance.

The importance of vengeance may be another one of those customs which have their origins in Gothic antecedents. Parkes has found that "in an effort to limit feuding, scales of wergild (blood-money) payments had been worked out, varying according to the rank of the victim; and the relatives might accept the appropriate sum in lieu of retaliatory killings. But they were not obliged to forgo vengeance, and incidents in the annals of the Dark Ages show that men were likely to develop uneasy consciences if they failed to exact a life for a life, feeling that to accept wergild was a mark of cowardice."[28]

I need not, however, insist on Gothic influence but may turn once again to Greek and Roman antecedents. To cite one example, Philip Vellacott writes in the introduction to his translation of Euripides' *The Bacchae* that the Chorus "sing of peace, justice, and the law of Heaven; but in a brief refrain they avow that for them the noblest of all things is the joy of revenge."[29] Another example may be found in Euripides' *Medea,* in which the Chorus promise Medea eventual justice from Zeus, but she insists that she must take part in the punishment by witnessing it here and now on earth: "With his bride *ere long may I see him* / In one ruin crushed with the house of her sire—/ They who unwronged find heart so to wrong me!" (italics mine).[30] Seneca's version of *Medea* presents an even stronger and more frequent emphasis on vengeance. It is, therefore, erroneous, I believe, to refer to the Valencians as followers of Seneca because of the bloodiness of their plots; rather we should speak of Seneca's influence as that of putting emphasis on the individual's need to exact vengeance, the bloodshed being a consequence, not an end.[31]

One of the few attempts to codify honor occurs in *Loyal Blood,* in which an effort is made to determine the origin of honor and once again we are shown the two sides of the coin. The king may create nobility or raise its status, a fact which Doña Lambra does not dispute. The two agree, then, that external recognition enhances honor, the king going so far as to suggest that before his intervention, Lambra's family honor was nothing since it was unseen. At this point, where the two sides of the coin converge, Lambra does not agree, referring to the king as merely the jeweler who polished the pure blood of the *old Christian,* which she had always preserved by her virtuous behavior. What this debate accomplishes, of course, is to provide a dual definition of honor: not honor *versus* reputation, but virtue *and* recognition as the two attributes which, when fused, result in honor. Moreover, the key to the origin and preservation of honor lies not merely in lineage or blood (whether bestowed by the

king or handed down by the *paterfamilias*) but in Fruela's ability to
fight and Lambra's capacity to resist. This codification is emphasized
by Lambra's highly significant assertion to the king that "our inherited nobility must be guarded with firmness." Nothing could be
more clearly designed to define honor as something which may be
inherited but which must be protected with firmness, that is, fortitude.

To sum up: the Valencian dramatists did not create a new genre
nor did they create a highly complex ethical code for a national
drama. But neither did Lope de Vega. On the other hand, when
Lope first set foot in Valencia, whether or not he had already written
his first, his tenth, or his hundredth *comedia*, he did not find virgin
territory. He found a thriving regional tradition with ideological
roots in antiquity. What Valencia lacked was not a code of ethics: it
had inherited that; what Valencia lacked was not a theatrical tradition: it had developed that; what Valencia lacked was not a set of
ingredients to convert classical tragedy into modern tragicomedy: it
was evolving in Valencia as well as elsewhere. What Valencia,
Seville, or Madrid lacked was a national stamp, a greater *poetic*
expression that would make the drama as inherited by Lope de Vega
and developed by him into a national genre, a part of world literature.

If I may close with some nonliterary analogies, Lope de Vega was
to the *comedia* what Verdi was to opera, what Caruso was to tenors,
what Babe Ruth was to baseball, what Richard Rodgers has been to
American musical comedy. Each of these individuals became
symbolic of the field in which they excelled, despite the fact that this
field existed before them and great individuals could still follow
them. What is unique about such people is their ability to use their
talents in such a way as to give it their own stamp and express the
emotions of the multitudes, so that it really did appear afterward
that they had created from dust. But dust forms the earth and it was
in the Valencian soil that Lope de Vega found much of what he was
able to convert into the national Spanish drama: the *comedia*.

Notes and References

Chapter One

1. The original Spanish is in the *Cancionero de la Academia de los Nocturnos de Valencia* (Valencia: Imprenta de Francisco Vives Mora, 1905), I, 11.

2. I use our word "dramatist," although during the period I am dealing with, the modern Spanish term *dramaturgo* was not in use, the Spaniards using *poeta dramático*, or "dramatic poet."

3. José Sánchez, *Academias literarias del Siglo de Oro español* (Madrid: Editorial Gredos, 1961), p. 223.

4. *Ibid.*, p. 225. Mercader was not a dramatist but a novelist, author of the pastoral novel *El Prado de Valencia*. However, *comedias* were apparently presented at his home if we are to believe the personages in Guillén de Castro's *Los mal casados de Valencia* who are off to see a *comedia* at the home of the *mercader* ("merchant"): "Which merchant?" / "Don Gaspar." See *Obras de Guillén de Castro*, ed. Eduardo Juliá Martínez, vol. II (Madrid: Real Academia Española, 1926), p. 475.

5. Juan Pérez de Guzmán, "Academias literarias de ingenios y señores bajo los Austrias," *La España Moderna* 6 (1894), 85.

6. Ludwig Pfandl, *Cultura y costumbres del pueblo español de los siglos XVI y XVII* (Barcelona: Casa Editorial Araluce, 1929), p. 183. His conclusion is supported by Alva V. Ebersole in his *Selección de comedias del Siglo de Oro español* (Madrid: Editorial Castalia, 1973), p. 31, who suggests that the *Academia de los Nocturnos* was perhaps the most famous of the literary academies of the Spanish Golden Age.

7. *Op. cit.*, p. 222.

8. Emilio Cotarelo y Mori, "La fundación de la academia española . . . ," *Boletín de la Real Academia Española* 1 (1914), 5.

9. *Ibid.*, p. 8.

10. J. L. Klein, *Geschichte des spanischen Dramas*, vol. III (Leipzig: T. O. Weigel, 1874), p. 638.

11. Henri Mérimée, *L'Art dramatique à Valencia* (Toulouse: Librairie Edouard Privat, 1913), p. 406. Unless otherwise noted, Mérimée's comments come from this work.

12. Klein (*loc. cit.*) claims that the academy lasted only until April 15, 1593, but I have been unable to find any justification for this date. Sánchez (p. 223) writes that the academy ceased to function in May, 1594, but on p. 226 agrees that the final year concluded on April 13, 1594.

13. *Op. cit.*, p. 184.

14. In his preliminary observations to his previously cited edition of the works of Guillén de Castro, I (1925), xiii.

15. *Op. cit.*, p. 227.

16. Cayetano Alberto de la Barrera y Leirado, *Catálogo bibliográfico y biográfico del teatro antiguo español* . . . (Madrid: M. Rivadeneyra, 1860), p. 323.

17. Francisco Martí Grajales, *Diccionario biográfico y bibliográfico de los poetas* . . . *de Valencia hasta el año 1700* (Madrid: Revista de Archivos, Bibliotecas y Museos, 1927), p. 377.

18. *Ibid.*, p. 387.

19. Eduardo Juliá Martínez, in his preliminary observations to his edition of *Poetas dramáticos valencianos* (Madrid: Real Academia Española, 1929), I, xxiv. Unless otherwise noted, Juliá's comments come from volume I of this edition.

20. *Op. cit.*, p. 435.

21. In a letter to me, Sánchez writes that he "never anticipated that this detail would become an issue" and that he "obviously . . . got that information from some source." Research on my part has failed to uncover this source. If correct, however, Sánchez' statement would mean that the *Academia de los Montañeses del Parnaso* was in existence before 1602, since there can be no doubt about the dates of the deaths of Artieda and Tárrega.

22. Juan Yagüe de Salas, *Los amantes de Teruel: epopeya trágica* (Teruel: Instituto de Estudios Turolenses, 1951), p. 601.

23. Domingo Gascón y Guimbao, ed., *Los amantes de Teruel* (Madrid: Imprenta de los Hijos de M. G. Hernández, 1907), p. 71.

24. *Op. cit.*, p. 228.

25. Froldi attributes the birth and rise of the academies, which he calls true meeting places of the intellectuals of the time, to the love for lyric poetry as a superior manifestation of spiritual elegance. See Rinaldo Froldi, *Lope de Vega y la formación de la comedia* (Salamanca: Ediciones Anaya, 1968), p. 51. Future references to Froldi come from this edition.

26. Froldi (*loc. cit.*) suggests that the failure to establish academies at the beginning of the seventeenth century is proof that tastes had already changed by then.

27. The Sargent book on Virués will be referred to in the chapter on that dramatist. The recent appearance of William E. Wilson's book, *Guillén de Castro*, in Twayne's World Authors Series (New York, 1973), is the principal reason for my not devoting a chapter to Castro. See the preface to the present book. The English translation of *The Youthful Deeds of the Cid* was published by Exposition Press (New York, 1969), translated by Robert R.

La Du, Luis Soto-Ruiz and Giles A. Daeger, with an introduction written by me. There exist, of course, a number of unpublished dissertations on several of the Valencian dramatists, particularly on Castro. Should any reader come upon Lord Holland's 1817 two-volume work entitled *Some Account of the Lives and Writings of Lope Felix de Vega Carpio and Guillén de Castro*, he will find precious little of Castro there.

28. Froldi, who also rejects the concept of a "school," nonetheless laments the scant attention paid by major works on the history of Spanish to the Valencian dramatists (p. 10). Hugo A. Rennert, in *The Spanish Stage in the Time of Lope de Vega* (New York: Hispanic Society of America, 1909), p. 192, actually says that Lope "was the founder of the Valencian School"!

29. Marcelino Menéndez y Pelayo, Introduction to vol. I of *Antología de poetas hispano-americanos* (Madrid: Real Academia Española 1893), p. lix.

30. Angel Valbuena Prat, *Literatura dramática española* (Barcelona: Editorial Labor, 1950), p. 173.

31. Angel Valbuena Prat, *Historia de la literatura española* (Barcelona: Editorial Gustavo Gili, S. A., 1964), II, 368.

32. Carlos [Karl] Vossler, *Lope de Vega y su tiempo* (Madrid: Revista de Occidente, 1940), p. 37.

33. Eduardo Juliá Martínez, *Lope de Vega y Valencia* (Madrid: C. Bermejo, 1935), pp. 5–6. Cf. S. Griswold Morley and Courtney Bruerton, *The Chronology of Lope de Vega's Comedias* (New York: Modern Language Association, 1940), p. 360. Lope's play is dated as 1586–95. Lope first arrived in Valencia in 1588.

34. Arnold G. Reichenberger, "The Uniqueness of the *Comedia*," *Hispanic Review* 27 (1959), 308. For a concise clarification of the honor concept, I refer the general reader to Wilson's *Guillén de Castro*, chapter 4.

35. P. N. Dunn, "Honour and the Christian Background in Calderón," in *Critical Essays on the Theatre of Calderón*, ed. Bruce W. Wardropper (New York: New York University Press, 1965), p. 46.

36. Jean Gagen, "Love and Honor in Dryden's Heroic Plays," *PMLA* 77 (1962), 209.

37. A. G. de Amezúa, *Cervantes, creador de la novela corta española*, vol. I (Madrid: Consejo Superior de Investigaciones Científicas, 1956), p. 201.

38. In his *Arte nuevo de hacer comedias en este tiempo* (New Art of Composing Plays in These Times). See the Bibliography in the final section of this book.

39. *Ibid*. The reference to the mixing of comic and tragic elements is made in Lope's *El laurel de Apolo*. See chapter 3.

40. S. G. Morley, "Strophes in the Spanish Drama Before Lope de Vega," in *Homenaje ofrecido a Menéndez Pidal* (Madrid, 1925), I, 523.

41. Manuel de Montoliu, *El alma de España y sus reflejos en la literatura del siglo de oro* (Barcelona: Editorial Cervantes, n.d.), p. 226.

42. Ebersole, *op. cit.*, p. 15.

43. Américo Castro, "La comedia clásica," in *El concepto contemporáneo de España* (Buenos Aires: Editorial Losada, 1946), p. 591.

44. See, for example, the intriguing remark by Ruth Lee Kennedy in "A Reappraisal of Tirso's Relations to Lope and his Theatre," *Bulletin of the Comediantes* 17 (1965), 33 n.: "Lope began to sense that theatrical winds were shifting as early as 1620, in which year he was evidently feeling the competition of Guillén de Castro (Valencian) and Mira de Amescua (Andalusian)."

45. It is Froldi's opinion that, without ignoring the existence or the importance of dramatic centers such as Madrid and Seville, it was in Valencia more than anywhere else that the structure of the *comedia* took shape and that it was in Valencia where Lope found it and gave it the impulse to reach its definitive triumph (p. 39).

Chapter Two

1. Alfredo Hermenegildo, *Los trágicos españoles del siglo XVI* (Madrid: Fundación Universitaria Española, 1961), p. 198.

2. Hermenegildo (*loc. cit.*) claims that Artieda was born in 1544 and not in 1549 as his biographers assert, but all the sources which I have consulted agree on 1549. Hermenegildo cites no documentation for his statement. Hermenegildo subsequently published *La tragedia en el renacimiento español* (Barcelona: Editorial Planeta, 1973), which, although it has a different, more mature, and more logical format, is fundamentally a revised and updated version of his earlier work. His insistence on 1544 as the correct date of Artieda's death is repeated in the very same words and much of what he has to say about Artieda and his work shows no change of importance other than to add references to scholars' comments made in the interim. On the other hand, his comments on Virués have an added perspective, as I shall note in chapter 3.

3. *Poetas dramáticos valencianos*, I, xxvi. Henceforth, unless otherwise noted, all lines attributed to the Valencian dramatists will be translated or paraphrased by me from this edition and the parentheses in the main text will indicate the volume (not the act) and page of this two-volume set for those wishing to seek the original Spanish.

4. *Op. cit.*, p. 12.

5. *Op. cit.*, p. 292. (The *Nises* were published in 1577.)

6. For bibliographies on the legend, see D. Gascón y Guimbao, *Los amantes de Teruel*, *ed. cit.*, and Emilio Cotarelo y Mori, *Sobre el origen y desarrollo de la leyenda de los amantes de Teruel* (Madrid: Revista de Archivos, Bibliotecas y Museos, 1907). See also the more recent *Los amantes de Teruel* (Teruel, 1958), edited by Gómez de Barreda.

7. See Cotarelo's work described in the preceding note, p. 82.

8. *Op. cit.*, p. 206.

9. *Ibid.*, p. 207.

10. *Sobre el origen* . . . , p. 35.

11. *Op. cit.*, pp. 310–11. Cf. Aristotle (*Poetics* 14.1): "Fear and pity may be aroused by spectacular means; but they may also result from the inner structure of the piece, which is the better way, and indicates a superior poet. For the plot ought to be so constructed that even without the aid of the eye, he who hears the tale told will thrill with horror and melt to pity at what takes place."

12. Ludwig Pfandl has noted that the death of the lovers is the logical end to the drama. See his *Historia de la literatura nacional española en la edad de oro* (Barcelona: Editorial Gustavo Gili, 1952), p. 125, where he explains that the fundamental tone of this truly human conflict, guided with beautiful coherence to the very end by Artieda, is the expiatory nature of the death of the lovers as the only solution to their courageous struggle.

13. The reference is to the well-known legend, originating in Greek mythology, of the lovers Hero and Leander. The latter swam the Hellespont (Dardanelles) each night to see his beloved Hero, guided by a light provided by her. One evening, the light blew out in a storm and Leander drowned. Hero, in despair, thereupon threw herself into the sea. The parallel with the Teruel legend is evident.

14. Even Hermenegildo, who objected to Artieda's portrayal of Sigura's character, sees a logical progression in the overall construction of the drama, pointing out that Artieda understood tragedy not as an accumulation of catastrophes at the end of the action but as a struggle of conflicting passions (*op. cit.*, p. 201).

15. Américo Castro, *De la edad conflictiva* (Madrid: Taurus Ediciones, 1961), pp. 56–57.

16. *Ibid.*, p. 72. I do not mean to imply that Américo Castro is among those who consider honor problems *per se* to originate with Lope. In fact, Castro was one of the first to note the equivalence of honor (*honra*) and reputation (*fama*) in the works of Torres Naharro, who antedated Lope by nearly three-quarters of a century. See Castro's "Algunas observaciones acerca del concepto del honor en los siglos XVI y XVII," *Revista de Filología Española* 3 (1916), 1–50, 357–76. However, in this article, Castro does claim that it was not until Lope's *comedias* that *fama* or what others think of someone is converted into the reason for human existence. That this concept is already present in *Los amantes* I shall attempt to show shortly. That honor is tied to *machez* or manliness is yet another "Lopean" concept that appears in *Los amantes*, as indicated earlier in the words of Marcilla himself.

17. Cf. Don Quixote's reaction to the dead body in chapter 19 of the first part of that work: "And who killed him?" Joaquín Casalduero's analysis of that question, namely, that it is unusual for a knight in the flower of his youth to die not in the battlefield but in bed (see his *Sentido y forma del Quijote* [Madrid: Ediciones Insula, 1949], p. 101), can be applied to the situation in *Los amantes* as well.

18. *Op. cit.*, pp. 543–44.

19. For those readers who are familiar with the Spanish language, I should make clear that my interpretation depends upon some editorial changes I have had to make in the text as edited by Juliá. In the first octave of Perafán's lament, the lines which I have translated as "That it can be that the course of life be cut short and interrupted . . . without a wound?" appear in the text as "¿Qué puede ser que ataje y que interrompa el curso . . . sin herida?" I am convinced that the accent mark on the first word is an error in view of the subjunctive of the two following verbs (*ataje* and *interrompa*). Perafán is not asking, after all, *what* kills a man in the flower of his youth. He knows it is Death and the entire stanza and much of the succeeding ones are devoted to his shock that Death can behave in such a manner.

Similarly, I have removed the question marks from the final line ("Fame revives and immortalizes"), which appears in Juliá's text as "¿ la fama lo reviva y eterniza?" Juliá evidently considered the word *consuélame* in the first line of this stanza (which I have translated as "I am consoled") to be an imperative, but this would not be consistent, since it would have Perafán requesting Death to console him with the information that Fame triumphs over Death. Mérimée (pp. 321–22) quotes these lines without the question marks and translates into French as follows: "Ma consolation du moins, c'est que votre complot ne fera oublier . . . les exploits de son bras . . . car ce que tu réduis en cendres, la renommée le ressuscite pour l'éternité." Mérimée also resolves the curious combination of subjunctive-indicative (*reviva* and *eterniza*) by considering the first indicative and making a phrase of the second.

There is only one extant manuscript of *Los amantes* (in the Biblioteca Nacional de Madrid), dating, of course, from 1581. In 1908 a reprinting was published but only fifty-one copies were made and none of these for public sale. Mérimée laments the careless editing of the 1908 version, presenting a sample of two lines which he considers representative (*las, de, cnito* for *los, do, cinto*). Juliá does not indicate which version he followed. Mérimée promised an annotated critical edition of *Los amantes*, but his untimely death prevented the completion of this enterprise.

20. "La vida / por la fama es bien perdida," See Joseph E. Gillet's edition of *Propalladia and Other Works of Bartolomé de Torres Naharro*, vol. II (Bryn Mawr: University of Pennsylvania Press, 1946), pp. 294–95.

21. The original can be found in *Cancionero castellano del siglo XV*, vol. II ("Nueva biblioteca de autores españoles," no. 21 [Madrid, 1915], p. 233).

22. Even today it is not uncommon to hear in our own Southwest, the complimentary description of a man as *muy macho* or *muy hombre*.

23. The Spanish word for "nobleman" is *hidalgo*, a contraction of *hijo de algo*, literally "son of something" or, more appropriately, "son of somebody who made something of himself."

24. Eduardo Juliá Martínez, "Nuevos datos sobre Micer Andrés Rey de Artieda," *Boletín de la Real Academia Española* 20 (1933), 667.

25. J. P. Wickersham Crawford, *Spanish Drama Before Lope de Vega*, revised edition (Philadelphia: University of Pennsylvania Press, 1967), p. 171.

26. John G. Weiger, "Tirso's Contribution in *Los amantes de Teruel*," *Bulletin of the Comediantes* 19 (1967), 33–35.

27. Charles V. Aubrun, *La comedia española* (Madrid: Taurus Ediciones, 1968), p. 113.

28. *Ibid.*, p. 153. Carmen I. de Ebersole, in "Andrés Rey de Artieda y *Los amantes de Teruel,*" *Hispanófila* 41 (1971), 13–21, gives examples of the seeds planted by Artieda not only for Tirso and Montalbán but for the *comedia* in general. Valbuena Prat, in *El teatro español en su Siglo de Oro* (Barcelona: Editorial Planeta, 1969), p. 78, suggests that since *Los amantes* was composed while Lope was in his teens, it is common sense to conclude that the way to Lope de Vega was already prepared.

29. Francisco Ruiz Ramón, *Historia del teatro español* (Madrid: Alianza Editorial, 1971), I, 115.

Chapter Three

1. The most complete study constitutes chapter 1 of Cecilia V. Sargent's *A Study of the Dramatic Works of Cristóbal de Virués* (New York: Instituto de las Españas, 1930). For a synthesis of the findings of Mérimée, Juliá, and Sargent, see Hermenegildo, *Los trágicos españoles del siglo XVI*, pp. 213–80.

2. See Sargent, pp. 2–3 n.

3. His brother, Jerónimo de Virués, was a member under the pseudonym of *Estudio* ("Study"). Ebersole (*op. cit.*, p. 75) considers the fraternal relationship sufficient to assume that Cristóbal must have attended several meetings of the academy.

4. "El Monserrate" is his monument in the field of epic poetry.

5. Ironically, Virués "expected his [own] verse to bring immortality to the friends it praised" (Sargent, p. 19). With regard to the three-act formula, Crawford (*Spanish Drama Before Lope de Vega*, ed. cit., p. 183) writes: "It is true that Avendaño's *Comedia Florisea*, in three acts, was printed in 1551, but the Spanish plays with which Virués was acquainted were written in four or rarely five acts, and he had good reasons to believe himself the inventor of a new form." Evidently, Lope de Vega believed it as well.

6. William C. Atkinson, "Séneca, Virués, Lope de Vega," in *Homenatge a Antoni Rubió i Lluch* (Barcelona: Estudis Universitaris Catalans, 1936), I, 111–31. As Hermenegildo points out in his 1973 edition of *La tragedia en el renacimiento español* (which, unlike his treatment given to Artieda, revises his views and adds new perspectives to the works of Virués), the works of Seneca were well known even in fifteenth-century Spain through Castilian,

Catalonian, or Italian versions. Seneca's presence is so strongly felt in this period of the sixteenth century, maintains Hermenegildo, that he is the support on which rests the bridge between Aristotle and Lope de Vega (p. 156). Atkinson's observation therefore adds to the importance of Virués in this evolutionary process. Although Hermenegildo chides Atkinson for making too much of what he, Hermenegildo, considers a narrow bond between Virués and Lope, he nonetheless follows this with his own conclusion that Virués was "the disciple of Seneca and the precursor of Lope as he fused in some complicated creations the old and the new" (p. 213).

7. *Ibid.*, p. 115. Atkinson is referring to the fact that the Spanish national drama, which we call the *comedia* is not really "comedy" but *tragicomedia* or "tragicomedy," a blending of tragic and comic elements, often in lower class parody scenes (comic) of upper class problems (tragic) and at other times a mixture of both simultaneously. This blend, typical of the Lopean *comedia*, would thus be ascribed by Lope himself to Virués' leadership.

8. *Ibid.*, p. 121.

9. *Ibid.*, p. 127.

10. I am following the order in which Virués' works appear in Juliá's edition. Although many critics believe *Elisa Dido* to have been written before the others because Virués followed classical models there, I tend to agree with Froldi (p. 112, n.59) that precisely because *Elisa Dido* has a format which is out of the ordinary, it could belong to any period of Virués' activity and be an isolated episode. What is more important, as Froldi suggests, is that Virués himself felt the need to point out the classical nature of *Elisa Dido* as something exceptional, "an undertaking foreign to his habitual interests" (p. 113) or, put another way, that his other works, which more closely resemble the structure of the baroque *comedia*, are those which we should consider typical of Virués' style.

11. Crawford, p. 164, after mentioning the handful of earlier tragedies of that century, primarily the two *Nises*, "for which their author, Fr. Jerónimo Bermúdez, justly claimed the title of *primeras tragedias españolas*" (p. 161).

12. This difference may account for the alternating approval and censure of Virués by the eighteenth-century neoclassicists.

13. Despite the pagan background of some of Virués' plays, Christian concepts abound. See Sargent, p. 45: "Even in the plays where the pagan subject-matter precludes direct expression of Christian sentiments, we find constant appeal to a righteous Providence which watches over and intervenes in the affairs of men, provided they forgive each other, obey their sovereign, and love and trust God." For a discussion of the "identity of *hados* with God's will," see Otis H. Green, *Spain and the Western Tradition*, vol. I (Madison: University of Wisconsin Press, 1963), pp. 156–57.

14. There is a Calderonian quality to these concepts, but the characters' response to them differs radically.

15. Here is a good example of what was soon to become a characteristic of

the "Lopean" *comedia:* the relationship of the particular circumstances in which a character finds himself to the general or universal principle involved, often expressed in aphorisms. See, for example, the study of R. D. F. Pring-Mill, "Sententiousness in *Fuente Ovejuna,*" *Tulane Drama Review* 7, no. 1 (1962), 5–37.

16. *Op. cit.,* p. 57. Note the almost incidental yet highly important connection made by Sargent between Dido's preservation of her chastity and her self-esteem, the latter a form of honor, the importance of which will be seen shortly.

17. See note 13 above.

18. As will be shown below, the attempt made to portray the heroine's death as an ascent to Heaven, cannot be applied to one whose behavior on earth has been vile and vicious.

19. Unlike *Elisa Dido,* which Virués considered "a tragedy in accordance with the old style" (I, 146), *La gran Semíramis* initiates the "new style" which, while it ignores the unities ("in three acts which occur in different times"), when one considers the play as a whole, may, when each act is viewed separately, be considered "as three tragedies, written not without art." The words quoted are translated from Virués' prologue, and it is in this same prologue, incidentally, that Virués boasts of the novelty of "the first play to be in three acts" (I, 25–26), which Lope substantiated in his *New Art.*

20. That the destructive power of love as one of the principal causes of man's miseries is a fundamental theme of Virués' works, has been clearly shown by Sargent.

21. Hermenegildo (p. 504), on summing up death in the sixteenth-century tragedy in general, chooses Menón as his example for the statement that "the desperate suicide of a character who has lost his reason to exist is frequent."

22. "What revelation of court habits of espionage when he unblinkingly explains to fellow-courtiers, 'acerqué los ojos / al agujero de la cerradura!' ['I put my eyes next to the keyhole!']" (Sargent, p. 67).

23. Atkinson (p. 124) considers her death the only justifiable one in the play: "If the lechery and over-reaching ambition of Semíramis justify the last death, two of the three are still void of purgative effect. The balance stands now at one-third pertinence, two-thirds gratuitous horror." However, I have already indicated the necessity for Menón's death. The nature of Nino's death will be discussed shortly. One must also bear in mind that beginning with this play, Virués' didacticism is of the "'by opposite example'" variety.

24. Guillén de Castro resolves a similar problem in his *El amor constante* by having the king give permission to Leonido to kill the man who affronted Leonido, even though it be the king himself. Since it was indeed the king who affronted him, Leonido takes advantage of the permission and kills him.

Although the killing of the king was considered nearly inconceivable (the great compilation of laws known as *Las siete partidas* describes fourteen ways of committing treason, regicide heading the list), I have shown elsewhere that it need not be considered revolutionary. See John G. Weiger, "Sobre la originalidad e independencia de Guillén de Castro," *Hispanófila* 31 (1967), 5–10. See also Hermenegildo's *La tragedia en el renacimiento español*, pp. 210–12.

25. As in the case of Semíramis and Nino, one cannot cite vengeance as the cause of Semíramis' murder by her son, despite Ninias' statement that he wishes to avenge the death of his father (I, 48), because again six years have elapsed since Nino's death. Moreover, Ninias' affection for his mother is evident (I, 47) until she reveals her perverse desires to him. Gwynne Edwards, in "Calderón's *La hija del aire* in the Light of His Sources," *Bulletin of Hispanic Studies* 43 (1966), 182, also concludes that it is Semíramis' "persistence in this direction [of desiring her own son as a lover] that leads [Ninias] to kill her."

26. *Op. cit.*, p. 37.

28. Semíramis herself never reveals her identity to Nino. After her departure, a servant tells him it was she.

28. *Op. cit.*, p. 65.

29. *Ibid.*, p. 48. Sargent apparently did not perceive the two types of exemplarity used by Virués, for after repeatedly stating that the destructive power of love is a fundamental theme and then considering Dido's case unique, she does note that with the exception of Dido, the female protagonists of Virués' plays "are unscrupulous, motivated by passion for vengeance; on the contrary, good women, including Dido, find their predominating motive in love." In all fairness, I must comment that such self-contradictory and ambiguous statements are not characteristic of Sargent's book.

30. That there is even more in common and of fundamental importance to a reexamination of the honor concept is described in the final chapter of this book. Dido's case, if I am correct, is not only *not* unique but quite consistent.

31. See Américo Castro, *loc. cit.*, in which he describes *buena fama* ("good fame" or "reputation," hence opposed to infamy) as being the patrimony of the privileged class, of the nobility; an *hidalgo*, is honorable *per se*. Honor in the nobleman, he maintains, is innate.

32. Cf. the previously cited comment by Sargent that Virués pictures "his heroes dupes of unscrupulous women."

33. That it became a commonplace is yet another indication of the Valencians' anticipating characteristics of the national *comedia*. Tirso de Molina was to be the one to employ this device most often. See M. Romera Navarro, "Las disfrazadas de varón en la comedia," *Hispanic Review* 2 (1934), 269–86. Also see, among others, Carmen Bravo-Villasante, *La mujer*

vestida de hombre en el teatro español (siglos XVI–XVII), (Madrid: Revista de Occidente, 1955) and Benjamin B. Aschcom, "Concerning 'la mujer en hábito de hombre en la comedia,'" *Hispanic Review* 28 (1960), 43–62. With regard to the Virués play in question, the interested reader will find food for thought in Daniel Rogers' "'¡Cielos! ¿Quién en Ninias habla?': The Mother-Son Impersonation in *La hija del aire*," *Bulletin of the Comediantes* 20 (1968), 1–4. Rogers observes that "the chief element in the plot [of Calderón's adaptation of the Virués work] . . . is the return to power of Queen Semíramis through her impersonation of her son. . . . .The extraordinary physical resemblance between the two is repeatedly remarked on . . . as [is] the *masculinity of the mother* . . . (p. 1; italics mine). Calderón, like Lope then, had but to take up where Virués had left off.

34. Cf. Azpilcueta, *Manual de confesores y penitentes* (first edition 1549): "If a woman dressed as a man . . . for just cause . . . she does not sin . . . ; nor does she do so more than venially if she does this out of . . . frivolity, without any other intention [in which case it] is mortal." Cited by Otis H. Green, *Spain and the Western Tradition,* I, 276.

35. Hermenegildo, *La tragedia en el renacimiento español,* p. 211. The article in question, titled "Adulación, ambición e intriga: los cortesanos de la primitiva tragedia española," finds parallels between these situations and the assassination of Juan de Escobedo, secretary to Don Juan of Austria, allegedly at the instigation of the princess of Eboli and by the hand of Antonio Pérez.

36. *Los trágicos españoles del siglo XVI,* p. 250.

37. *Op. cit.,* p. 116.

38. Adolf Schaeffer, *Geschichte des spanischen National-dramas* (Leipzig: F. A. Brockhaus, 1890), I, 69.

39. The earlier version, revised by Crawford himself, is from 1937 and the sentence is found on p. 184. The 1967 version, issued after Crawford's death and under the supervision of Warren T. McCready (and unless otherwise specified is the edition referred to in this book), has already been alluded to in the previous chapter. The quotation in my text comes from p. 185 of this edition.

40. Jean-Louis Flecniakoska, "L'Horreur morale et l'horreur matérielle dans quelques tragédies espagnoles du XVI⁰ siècle," in *Les Tragédies de Sénèque et le théâtre de la Renaissance* (Paris: Editions du Centre National de la Recherche Scientifique, 1964), p. 72.

41. Sargent, p. 99, calls him "a monstrosity rather than a personality."

42. *Op. cit.,* I, 17.

43. *Ibid.*

44. In the original Spanish, Atila is repeatedly referred to in the drama as the *açote de Dios.* Most dictionaries explain this meaning of *açote* (modern spelling: *azote*) by citing Atila (Atilla). There exists also a play by Luis Vélez de Guevara entitled *Atila, azote de Dios.*

45. "The most severe punishment [in the Golden Age drama] is damnation, consignment to hell" (A. A. Parker, *The Approach to the Spanish Drama of the Golden Age* [London: The Hispanic and Luso-Brazilian Councils, 1957], p. 7). Cf. Revelation 20:14, "And death and hell were cast into the lake of fire. This is the second death."

46. The general concept that honor depends on virtue is already present in Aristotle, as Virués himself points out in this same prologue: "Aristotle says that one ought to embrace virtue with more affection than one's dear husband or flushed lover, sweet wife or beloved lady" (I, 58). I believe that the analysis which I attempt in chapter 9 of this book will provide a clarifying context for such a statement.

47. *De la edad conflictiva*, p. 62. This is the advice offered to and accepted by the king in Guillén de Castro's *The Youthful Deeds of the Cid* with regard to the famous slap administered in his presence. The principle of a secret vengeance for an unpublicized affront was to become a characteristic of some of Calderón's *comedias*.

48. *Op. cit.*, p. 126. Cf. his statement on p. 125: "Pertinence, nought; gratuitous horror, the lot." Pointing out the lack of tragic elements in *Atila* and *Casandra*, Atkinson observes that "as each husband is himself guilty of infidelity . . . we withhold assent from the tragic inevitability of the fates of his victims." Were I to substitute "exemplarity" for "tragic inevitability," my own view would be more closely expressed.

49. One notes here a combination of Nino's lust and Menón's rejection of duty (*La gran Semíramis*).

50. The reference to points made earlier is clear: the warning alludes to the kind of honor which is innate in the noble and which no kind of ritualistic deeds can create. The interesting point, and highly significant for the conclusions reached in the final chapter is that by not *behaving* like a gentleman, even that kind of honor which is born with him may be lost.

51. *Op. cit.*, p. 107.

52. It may seem odd that a bandit should be affronted by the actions of a nobleman, in which case we would have here an antecedent of the Peribáñez-Comendador situation in Lope's *Peribáñez*. However, Formio is actually of noble blood himself. See John G. Weiger, "Nobility in the Theater of Virués," *Romance Notes* 7 (1966), 180–82. See also J. R. Hale, *Renaissance Europe* (New York: Harper and Row, 1971), p. 26: "The bandits who swept down on travellers and held villages to ransom were not only the detritus of war but the waste products of de-feudalisation and a closening contact between government and society as a whole." Hermenegildo's 1973 revision of his 1961 book takes no notice of my 1966 article and simply restates his surprise at the courtly language employed by the bandits when they address Formio (*La tragedia en el renacimiento español*, p. 265).

53. The poison taken by Marcela had been intended by Formio to give Felina a peaceful death: "Felina cannot complain about me; I'm giving her a gentle and peaceful death" (I, 142).

54. *Op. cit.*, p. 127.

55. The association of marriage with death is not uncommon in the *comedia*. Cf. John G. Weiger, "Matrimony in the Theatre of Guillén de Castro," *Bulletin of the Comediantes* 10 (1958), 1–3.

56. *Op. cit.*, p. 143. Valbuena Prat (*El teatro español en su Siglo de Oro*, p. 75) calls Virués the most patent case of the fusion of the classical or ancient art with the free way of those who shut the precepts under lock and key. (The reference is to Lope's *New Art*, which advised the classical precepts to be locked up with six keys.)

57. *Ibid.* The reference is to Frederick Bouterwek's *History of Spanish and Portuguese Literature*, translated by T. Ross (London, 1823), I, 442–46, as described in Sargent's bibliography (p. 160), but the note itself gives the title, date, and pagination as *History of Spanish Literature* (London, 1847), p. 313 ff. (Sargent, p. 143). The curious bibliographer can find the clarification in entry number 7 of Homero Serís' *Manual de bibliografía de la literatura española* (Syracuse: Centro de Estudios Hispánicos, 1948).

58. Sargent, pp. 153–54.

59. *Op. cit.*, p. 184.

60. *Op. cit.*, p. 155. On the role of Juan de la Cueva, see Froldi, who denies him the position of Lope's forerunner. See especially pp. 103–9 of Froldi's book. However, see also Humberto López Morales, *Tradición y creación en los orígenes del teatro castellano* (Madrid: Ediciones Alcalá, 1968), p. 24 n., who suggests that Lope's silence on Juan de la Cueva was a weapon and that Virués merely took Cueva's place for that reason in the reference in *El laurel de Apolo!* This, incidentally, is the only mention of Virués or the other Valencians in a book devoted to the origins of Castilian theater.

Chapter Four

1. Ramón de Mesonero Romanos, ed., *Dramáticos contemporáneos a Lope de Vega* (Madrid: M. Rivadeneyra, 1857), p. xx.

2. *Op. cit.*, p. 380.

3. *Op. cit.*, p. 434.

4. *Op. cit.*, p. 31.

5. *Op. cit.*, I, 237.

6. J. Serrano Cañete, *El canónigo Francisco Agustín Tárrega, poeta dramático del siglo XVI* (Valencia: El Archivo, 1889), p. 10.

7. *Loc. cit.*

8. *Loc. cit.* (Also cited by Froldi, p. 118.)

9. Martí Grajales, *loc. cit.*

10. *Ibid.* Doctor Virués is, of course, Jerónimo Virués, brother of the dramatist Cristóbal.

11. Quoted by Martí Grajales, p. 435. See also Cervantes' Prologue to his own eight *comedias*, in which he praises Tárrega, as well as the specific praise of Tárrega's *La enemiga favorable* in *Don Quixote*, I, 48.

12. *Ibid.*

13. Juliá, *Lope de Vega y Valencia*, pp. 3–4.

14. Cf. the review by Joseph G. Fucilla of the original Italian version of Froldi's *Il teatro valenzano e l'origine della commedia barocca* (Pisa: Editrice Tecnico-Scientifica, 1962) in *Hispania* 47 (1964), 866–67: "The most important of the three [Artieda, Virués and Tárrega] is Tárrega . . . and in his *Prado de Valencia* (1577) he sees a genuine exemplar in the genre as to theme, *sentimiento de honor*, language, double plot, a *lacayo* who resembles the *gracioso*, versification."

15. Joseph E. Gillet, *Torres Naharro and the Drama of the Renaissance* (Philadelphia: University of Pennsylvania Press, 1961), p. 520.

16. Rather than as a consequence of the difference between two ages, as Gillet had concluded (Green, *op. cit.*, I, 122).

17. The exact date and whether *El Prado de Valencia* was or was not Tárrega's first play, have not yet been settled and scholars have gone from one extreme to another. Mérimée (p. 519) indicates that it was indeed the first and fixes its date of composition as 1589. Serrano Cañete (*op. cit.*, p. 40) believes the date to have been 1588. Courtney Bruerton, in his "La versificación dramática española en el período 1587–1610," *Nueva Revista de Filología Hispánica* 10 (1956), 337–64, dates it 1590. Froldi makes a serious attempt to show that two other plays antedate *El Prado* (pp. 119–20), which would make *El Prado* the third play to be written (or perhaps the fourth, since one page later, Froldi decides to add another play to the first stage of Tárrega's productivity). Yet, on p. 125, Froldi makes the significant statement, cited earlier, that "Tárrega truly initiates what we call the Spanish *comedia*, "which is immediately followed by the observation that "*El Prado de Valencia* appears to be a sure and *mature* work . . ." (italics mine). I cannot, incidentally, account for Fucilla's date in his review of this very paragraph when he cites 1577 as the year of composition. See note 14.

18. It is a commonplace in the *comedia* that if a lady accepted letters from a gentleman, this was sufficient to compromise her. See, for example, act I of Lope de Vega's *El remedio en la desdicha*, act II of Tirso de Molina's *El burlador de Sevilla*, act I of *La prueba de las promesas*, act I of *El semejante a sí mismo*, act III of *La verdad sospechosa* (all by Alarcón), and act I of Calderón's *La devoción de la cruz*.

19. Laura's ignorance of the exigencies and nature of society at the beginning of the play constitutes her "comic flaw." For a discussion of this element in the *comedia*, see Irving P. Rothberg, "El agente cómico de Lope de Vega," *Hispanófila* 16 (1962), 69–90. See also Bruce W. Wardropper, "Lope's *La dama boba* and Baroque Comedy," *Bulletin of the Comediantes* 13 (1961), 1–3, which describes perfectly the circumstances found in *El Prado de Valencia*. Wardropper points out that comedy, as opposed to the serious drama, deals with unmarried people, learning to cope with the problems of life and society, whose failings can be considered funny, and

hence we can laugh at them. Their problem is to learn "to live with the insubstantial shadow of a substantial reality which may be realized in the future" (p. 2), and their lovemaking "is seen as a learning process, a preparation in deceptive conditions for a married life in which deceit may have no place. . . . [The heroine] learns to accept [the deceptions of life], recognizing that it is but a transitory stage on the road to the moral rectitude that will be hers with marriage" (p. 3).

20. Although Froldi includes the honor motif among his list, I do not agree with his qualification that honor does not come forth with the sharpness that will be characteristic of the seventeenth-century theater. The attempt to explain this apparent difference in note 88 of that page does not sound convincing to me either (viz., that it corresponds to Tárrega's particular psychology and morality), but these are elements to which I shall return in the concluding chapter.

21. At first blush this may seem to be our modern (and Christian) view that honor and virtuous deeds are valuable because of the philanthropic aspects of honorable behavior. However, we can go back to Cicero's *De Officiis* to read that "indifference to public opinion implies not merely self-sufficiency, but even total lack of principle." (As translated by Walter Miller in the Loeb Classical Library [Cambridge: Harvard University Press, 1956], 1:28.)

22. If the marquis is referring to honor and glory as *worldly* goods, he is undoubtedly correct. If he is neglecting the "other, better, glorious life of honor," he has misunderstood the meaning of the swan's song. Cf. Plato, *Phaedo*, 85e: ". . . when these birds [swans] feel that the time has come for them to die, they sing more loudly and sweetly than they have sung in all their lives before, for joy that they are going away into the presence of the god whose servants they are. It is quite wrong for human beings to make out that the swans sing their last song as an expression of grief at their approaching end. . . . I believe that the swans, belonging as they do to Apollo, have prophetic powers and sing because they know the good things that await them in the unseen world, and they are happier on that day than they have ever been before."

23. I obviously disagree with Froldi's sweeping statement that "the plot of *Las suertes trocadas* is totally comic," as well as with his failure to spot the importance of the madness of the count and the student, all of which Froldi includes among the abundant farcical scenes of the play (p. 123).

24. Again, I cannot agree with Froldi when he concludes that this work is an "explicit renunciation on the literary side of the grave tones of an Artieda or of a Virués" (p. 124).

25. Such an attitude toward bigamy would hardly be consistent in the Canon's "psychology" if I were to accept Froldi's analysis of such matters as discussed in note 20 above. That it was bigamy in appearance only is revealed in Teodosia's comment, quoted in the text, that she did not permit

the consummation of the marriage. Such devices, which at first blush seem shocking, were rare but not unheard of. See, for example, my previously cited article on the originality of Guillén de Castro in which I deal briefly with his *Los malcasados de Valencia* (The Ill-Marrieds of Valencia), a play which many scholars found opposed to the times, shocking and even revolutionary, because it ends in the divorce of all the parties. Yet, a careful reading reveals that they were not properly married in the first place, hence no true divorce. Tárrega is employing a similar recourse here and both Valencian dramatists give much away in the titles of the two plays. Froldi, p. 123, is correct but misses the inner significance when he dismisses the play as an apparent tragedy which turns out to be pure comedy. Gerald E. Wade's review of Hesse's *La Comedia y sus intérpretes,* in the *Bulletin of the Comediantes* 26 (1974), p. 35, applies here. Wade points out that "tragedy" and "comedy" cannot as yet be defined with finality, adding, "Recently there has been increasing effort by scholars to explicate comedy more carefully than heretofore; the effort is especially pertinent because as a genre the *comedia* is nearly all comedy rather than tragedy (the terms are used here in their conventional meanings)."

26. That love is based on one's will and that forced or arranged marriages are undesirable are concepts that are frequently repeated in Tárrega's works. For example, in *The Meadow of Valencia,* we are told that "in love's law, one does not conquer a favor by force nor by deceit (I, 187), and in *Reversed Fortunes,* Maurelia objects to her father's having promised her to the marquis because "where there is no will, marrying is losing your mind" (I, 391). In *The Siege of Rhodes,* Don Gonzalo promises to force his brother to keep his promise of marriage to Doña Blanca, but she refuses to enter into matrimony on these terms because "it is with force and doesn't please me, for never did a hand of love go well with an armed hand" (I, 284). Here again, Tárrega was followed repeatedly by his younger countryman, Guillén de Castro, as I have attempted to demonstrate on several occasions. See the Bibliography.

27. Wardropper, *op. cit.,* p. 1.

28. Ganimedes, a fisherman, had lied to the duke, claiming to have been a witness to Flaminia's dishonor. His motive was to help Torcato's wife in the hope that the duke would punish Torcato. Tirsia, Ganimedes' wife, then made her husband tell the duke the truth about Flaminia, making the comment cited in the text in answer to Ganimedes' objection that it no longer mattered since Flaminia was dead.

29. George T. Northup, ed., *Three Plays by Calderón* (Boston: D. C. Heath, 1926), p. xvii.

30. Robert R. La Du, "Honor and the King in the *Comedias* of Guillén de Castro," *Hispania* 45 (1962), 215.

31. *Ibid.,* p. 216.

32. P. W. Bomli, *La Femme dans l'Espagne du siècle d'or* (La Haye: Martinus Nijhoff, 1950), p. 69.

33. *Ibid.*, p. 70.

34. That is, she is unable to meet her obligations of honor. "To have blood in one's eye" (*tener sangre en el ojo*) means to have honor enough to comply with one's obligations in accordance with one's duties (cited from the *Diccionario de Autoridades* by Víctor Said Armesto, ed., *Las mocedades del Cid* by Guillén de Castro [Madrid, 1952], pp. 38–39 n.).

35. *Op. cit.*, I, 18.

36. This is the principle of *las blancas manos no ofenden* (white [feminine] hands do not offend) described by Northup, p. xxi.

37. I am guided here by A. A. Parker, *op. cit.*, p. 6: "The relation of theme to action has nothing whatever to do with the degree of verisimilitude in the latter, but depends entirely upon analogy. The plot of a play is merely an invented situation, and as such a kind of metaphor since its contact with reality is not that of literal representation but analogical correspondence; the theme of a play is the human truth expressed metaphorically by the stage fiction. . . . It does not matter in the least if the plot of a play is untrue to life in the sense of being untrue to normal experience. . . ."

38. Juliá notes that for Tárrega, "the problem of veracity was secondary" (p. lxxxviii).

39. Juliá calls it the *comedia* in which Tárrega managed best to express deep feelings, present moments of pathos and develop the plot with greatest expertise (p. xc). Mérimée qualifies his praise with a desire for less obscurity, in which case, he says, it would certainly be the poet's masterpiece, as much because of the height of the play's conception as because of the pathos of the situations (p. 477). As mentioned earlier, Froldi reserves his greatest praise for *El Prado de Valencia*, barely mentioning *La sangre leal*. Ebersole, in his anthology cited earlier, explains that his two reasons for selecting *El Prado* are Froldi's evaluation and the fact that it is the play by Tárrega most often cited by critics.

40. This is the thesis which appears repeatedly in the works of Américo Castro. See, for instance, his *La realidad histórica de España* (Mexico: Editorial Porrúa, 1962), p. 142 and his *De la edad conflictiva*, p. 98.

41. Cf. the similar attitude of Juan Labrador in Lope de Vega's *El villano en su rincón*, act I: "Heaven, I give you the most overwhelming thanks, because you have given me happiness in the state in which you have put me. I seem to be a man quite opposite to the courtly one, sad because of honors and ambitions, who adorns his heart and mind with so many passions, because I, without a worry about honor, live honorably with my equals."

42. *Op. cit.*, p. 213. La Du points out that a man would normally "not ask the king to intervene in an affair of honor, for the code demanded that an individual take vengeance personally" (p. 212) and hence he would feel "loath to permit anyone—even the king—to take vengeance for him unless it were quite impossible to avenge the affront personally" (p. 213).

43. In Guillén de Castro's *The Youthful Deeds of the Cid* (with which this play has many elements in common), Diego feels a similar rejuvenation after Rodrigo kills the count who had slapped Diego in front of *his* king.

44. Alfredo Lefebvre, *La fama en el teatro de Lope* (Madrid: Taurus Ediciones, 1962), p. 7.

45. Speaking of Torres Naharro's *Comedia Serafina*, Green summarizes his own completion of Gillet's analysis as follows: "There has been no actual death, but there need not be. The substitute for death . . . is . . . spiritual as against physical punishment, utter confusion, complete loss of reality. . . . This replacing of death by confusion and loss of identity will have a fruitful development in Spain's classic drama of the seventeenth century. Its appearance here, before 1520, constitutes a noteworthy landmark." See Otis H. Green, "Imaginative Authority in Spanish Literature," *PMLA* 84 (1969), 212. Ironically, Green presented this paper at the same 1968 MLA meetings during which I read my "The Shadow of Death in the *Comedias* of Tárrega," alluded to in the preface. Since Professor Green was among my listeners, I am somewhat disappointed that he continues to leave the hiatus between 1520 and the seventeenth century.

46. *Op. cit.*, p. 7.

47. *Ibid.*

48. *Op. cit.*, p. 867.

49. Ebersole, pp. 12–13.

Chapter Five

1. Emiliano Diez-Echarri y José María Roca Franquesa, *Historia de la literatura española e hispanoamericana* (Madrid: Aguilar, 1960), p. 488.

2. *Op. cit.*, p. 13.

3. Henri Mérimée, "Sur la biographie de Gaspar Aguilar," *Bulletin Hispanique*, 8 (1906), 396.

4. The details of this homage may be found in Martí Grajales, pp. 19–20.

5. It is difficult to justify the title of this play. The heroine, Irene, is described in the list of characters and in the opening scene as a gypsy. No further reference to her being a gypsy is made. In fact, we learn that she is the illegitimate daughter of the Roman emperor and that her mother, now deceased, was queen of Egypt. Mérimée comments that we might like it better if it bore another title (p. 497).

6. This is the *palabra de esposo* ("promise to wed"), of which there were two varieties: *in verbis de futuro* ("I shall take thee to my wife"), which was not considered binding; and *in verbis de praesenti* ("I do take thee"), which was considered as more important than the marriage ceremony itself. See Carroll Camden, *The Elizabethan Woman* (Houston: The Elsevier Press, 1952), pp. 86 ff.

7. The proper waiting time was one year. See *Las siete partidas*, IV, title XII, law iii; see also the Archpriest Juan Ruiz, *Libro de buen amor* (Book of

Good Love), stanza 759. In the *comedia*, see, for example, Tirso de Molina's *La prudencia en la mujer* (Prudence in Woman), act I, in which the queen is furious at the suggestion that she remarry shortly after her husband's death because "in tearful widowhood the most ordinary woman keeps her respect for the most cruel husband for a year."

8. Cf. Tárrega's *El esposo fingido*, in which the fact that the poison turned out to be a sleeping potion was similarly interpreted as God's will.

9. Henry N. Bershas, "The Source of Gaspar Aguilar's *La venganza honrosa*," *Romance Notes* 8 (1967), 269.

10. Curtis B. Watson, in his *Shakespeare and the Renaissance Concept of Honor* (Princeton: Princeton University Press, 1960), p. 92, quotes the seventeenth-century English moralist Bryskett as typical of a distinction repeatedly made between those who are motivated "for vertues sake, for feare of reproch, for love and reverence to honestie" and those who are moved "for feare of punishment to be inflicted on them by the magistrates."

11. Angel Valbuena Briones, *Perspectiva crítica de los dramas de Calderón* (Madrid: Ediciones Rialp, S. A., 1965), pp. 35–53.

12. Cf. Guillén de Castro's *El perfecto caballero* (The Perfect Gentleman): "Money doesn't add quality, although it provides advantages."

13. See note 23 to chapter 2.

14. Cf. Don Quixote's explanation of the two types of lineage: ". . . there are two kinds of lineage in the world: some, which bring and derive their descendence from princes and monarchs, whom the world has undone little by little and who have ended up in a tip, like an inverted pyramid; others had their beginning from low-class people, and are gradually rising degree by degree until they get to be great lords." Sancho Panza's reply expresses the attitude of D. García in Aguilar's play: "I am an old Christian, and in order to be a count, that's enough for me" (*Don Quixote*, I, 21). It comes as no surprise, then, that Cervantes praised *El mercader amante* in *Don Quixote*, I, 48.

Chapter Six

1. *Op. cit.*, p. 47.

Chapter Seven

1. Martí Grajales, (p. 58), has reproduced the *Legitimación de don Carlos Boyl* from the *Archivo General del Reino de Valencia*.

2. As well as Boil, there was another member of the academy with the same pseudonym whose real name was Francisco de Villanova. Sánchez (pp. 225–26) lists both *Recelos* without comment. Martí Grajales (p. 54), although he refers to Villanova as a "completely unknown Valencian talent," thinks that he belonged to the academy prior to Boil's admittance, for he mentions that our poet's pseudonym was the same as that which Villanova had used "previously." I might recall at this point that Boil later founded his

own *Academia de los Adorantes*, but, as I pointed out in chapter 1, we possess barely any information concerning this literary group.

3. The proper account of Boil's death is accurately recorded by Martí Grajales, *loc. cit.*: Around the end of November, 1617, in the vicinity of the cathedral and perhaps as the result of some amorous intrigue, a stranger struck him a blow, leaving him seriously wounded. He was taken to a nearby house and a few days later, on December 8, he passed away. On the following day he was buried in the church of the convent of *Predicadores de Santo Domingo*. Martí Grajales also reproduces on p. 59 of his work the death certificate, dated 1617, in which it is written that Boil died on December 8.

Juliá, however, gives the following description: On August 19, 1618, at the exit of the cathedral, Boil was the victim of an ambush, being so seriously wounded that he could not be taken to his house. He made his testament on November 25 and died on December 8, being buried the following day (p. cxxi). Not only does this give Boil one more year of life, but it would lead one to believe that he received his fatal wound in August and did not succumb until more than three months later.

The confusion is cleared when we recall that Juliá's major source is Mérimée, who, after giving a list of Boil's children, continues by saying that when the last one was baptized on August 19, 1618, his playboy father had already found in an ambush the only death which befitted him. In the vicinity of the cathedral, in the last days of November, 1617, he received a blow from a sword by an unknown adversary which left him hanging between life and death for two weeks. From the first moment he was faltering so badly that it was judged impossible to take him home; in a neighboring house he made his testament and on December 8 he died (p. 639).

Evidently Juliá read this passage hurriedly, confusing the baptismal date of Boil's child (August 19, 1618) with that of the attack (November, 1617). Martí Grajales, *loc. cit.*, has reproduced the baptismal certificate of Boil's youngest child, which verifies that the baptism was performed in the year following Boil's death.

4. *Op. cit.*, p. xxvii.

5. Hymen Alpern, "Jealousy as a Dramatic Motive in the Spanish 'Comedia,'" *Romanic Review* 14 (1923), 283.

6. *Ibid.*, p. 281.

Chapter Eight

1. *Op. cit.*, p. xxiii. Mesonero believed Turia to have been the poet D. Luis Ferrer, who died in 1641.

2. Martí Grajales, p. 372.

3. As in Artieda's *Los amantes*, I have had to make some changes in the punctuation. The original Spanish reads:

> *el morir es posible que os espante,*
> *y ¿no os tiene el servir amedrentados?*
> *Como la muerte no es, cuando es honrosa,*
> *más que la esclavitud dulce y sabrosa.*

As written, the last two lines distort the sense as I interpret it, for they would have to be translated to read "As death is not, when it is honorable, sweeter and more savory than slavery." This would indicate a syntactical flaw, for one would expect a comma at the end, followed by a concluding clause. Moreover, it would have Lautaro saying that an honorable death is not more pleasant than slavery. That he does not believe this is evidenced by his subsequent cry of encouragement to his fellow Indians as he says "I die joyfully for my country."

Gerald E. Wade, in "'El burlador de Sevilla': Some Annotations," *Hispania* 47 (1964), 759, points out "the probability that almost any line that fails to make sense has been changed from its original." I believe that such is the case here and to restore the sense, my translation is based on surrounding the sentence under discussion with question marks and placing the required accent mark on the initial word. Thus, following the question of amazement in the previous lines, Lautaro expresses further disbelief, as indicated in my translation.

It is also be possible to punctuate these lines as follows:

> *el morir, ¿es posible que os espante?*
> *y, ¿no os tiene el servir amedrentados?*
> *¡Cómo! La muerte no es, cuando es honrosa,*
> *más que la esclavitud dulce y sabrosa.*

I am indebted to Professor Walter Poesse for this possible punctuation, as well as his alternate interpretation, which would have the final sentence meaning, "Death, when it is an honorable one, is only a sweet and savory servitude."

4. That this attitude is not new can be seen in, among many other places, Chaucer's "The Physician's Tale," one of the *Canterbury Tales*, which in turn was not original with Chaucer.

Chapter Nine

1. *De Officiis*, 1:43. While it is true that Aristotle antedates Cicero in the definition of honor as a reward for virtue, the statement I cite by Cicero is much closer to a description of the nature of that virtue and the conflict that would make true drama of the need to preserve these bases of virtue which in turn was the source of honor in its inner *and* outer forms.

It might be argued that even before Aristotle, Plato had attempted to define the several virtues and even to distinguish between behavior and reputation. Although this is true, particularly in *Republic*, the metaphysical dialogues are not as directly related to my study as are the more concrete definitions of Aristotle and more particularly, Cicero and Seneca. There is, nevertheless, one highly interesting statement in Plato's *Protagoras*, 324d–325b: "Is there or is there not some one thing in which all citizens must share, if a state is to exist at all? . . . If there is, and this one essential is not the art of building or forging or pottery but justice and moderation and holiness of life, *or to concentrate it into a whole, manly virtue . . .* , then think what extraordinary people good men must be!" (italics mine).

2. Watson, *op. cit.*, p. 66. Subsequent references to Watson come from this edition.

3. Eric Partridge, *Origins: A Short Etymological Dictionary of Modern English* (New York: The Macmillan Co., 1959), p. 783.

4. See, however, Américo Castro, *La realidad histórica de España*, especially the fifth chapter entitled "There Weren't Yet Any Spaniards in Roman or Visigothic Hispania" (translation mine), which insists that Seneca cannot be considered a Spaniard.

5. Neal Wood, "Some Common Aspects of the Thought of Seneca and Machiavelli," *Renaissance Quarterly* 21 (1968), 15.

6. *Ibid.*, pp. 16–17.

7. *The Stoic Philosophy of Seneca*, translated by Moses Hadas (Garden City: Doubleday Anchor Books, 1958), p. 174.

8. *Ibid.*, p. 36.

9. *Ibid.*, p. 32.

10. Américo Castro, *Hacia Cervantes* (Madrid: Taurus, 1957), p. 57.

11. Germán Orduna, "Las *Coplas* de Jorge Manrique y el triunfo sobre la muerte: Estructura e intencionalidad," *Romanische Forschungen* 79 (1967), 149. The reference to Pedro Salinas is his *Jorge Manrique o tradición y originalidad.* See the Bibliography.

12. Otis H. Green, "Imaginative Authority in Spanish Literature," p. 212.

13. R. N. Shervill, "Lope's Ways with Women," *Bulletin of the Comediantes* 15 (1963), 10. In addition to the arguments made in my text concerning the fortitude of women in the *comedia*, a good deal of evidence exists that successful plays depended upon the willingness of outstanding actresses to play significant roles, hence the need for dramatic or heroic parts for them. The situation is not much altered in our own day, whether in the films or on the Broadway stage. For evidence on the *comedia*'s need for such actresses, see Sturgis E. Leavitt, "Spanish *Comedias* as Pot Boilers," *PMLA* 82 (1967), 181–83. See also Watson's observation that "a woman's 'honor' and 'honesty,' in the 16th century, consisted almost exclusively in the preservation of her virginity as long as she was unmarried and in her faithfulness to her husband after marriage" (p. 159), followed by his ag-

reement that "it would be an exaggeration to say that [woman] was never considered capable of heroic actions" (p. 161).

An interesting light is shed on this ideology from a totally different viewpoint in the recent canonization of the first American-born saint, Mother Seton. During the long process which culminated in sainthood in 1974, Pope John XXIII in 1959 declared that Mother Seton had exhibited the "heroicity of virtues" required of a saint. See *The New York Times*, Dec. 10, 1974, p. 46. Even those virtues of saintly behavior, then, are regarded as having heroic aspects.

14. *La tragedia en el renacimiento español*, p. 483.

15. *Ibid.*, p. 254. I have already alluded to Hermenegildo's basis for his own interpretation (see note 35 to chapter 3). His in no way invalidates my own, since, if he is correct, Virués made use of his personal viewpoints within a larger context of the virtuous and virile woman. The two concepts, incidentally, can be traced as far back as the Bible. See Proverbs 31:10–31.

16. *Ibid.*, p. 213.

17. This is definition no. 5 from *The Oxford Universal Dictionary on Historical Principles*, third edition, revised with addenda (London: Oxford University Press, 1955). The dates in the quotation indicate the earliest known occurrence of the particular definition.

18. Rudolf Dreikurs, "Are Psychological Schools of Thought Outdated?" *Journal of Individual Psychology*, 16 (1960), 3.

19. More surprising is to find Hermenegildo (*La tragedia en el renacimiento español*) maintaining that Virués *headed* the movement when on p. 35 he had linked Artieda with Virués and Cervantes as *stragglers* (in Spanish, *rezagados*), defeated dramatists who struggled in their discontent against the new school! The fact that some 160 pages later these words are ascribed to Menéndez Pelayo (p. 196) does not invalidate Hermenegildo's inconsistency.

20. Interestingly, La Barrera, in his previously cited dictionary, refers in the entry on Aguilar to "the distinguished school where later the great Lope de Vega Carpio perfected his taste."

21. Margaret Wilson, *Spanish Drama of the Golden Age* (Oxford: Pergamon Press Ltd., 1969), p. 53.

22. "Imaginative Authority in Spanish Literature," p. 212. See my previous comment to note 45 of chapter 4.

23. Edwin S. Morby, review of Froldi's *Il teatro valenzano e l'origine della commedia barocca*, *Hispanic Review* 32 (1964), 266.

24. See Juliá's review of Froldi's Italian version in *Revista de Literatura* 21 (1962), 181–83. Juliá concludes that the *comedia* received its nourishment from the Valencian tradition and that the poets of Valencia contributed to the formative years of Lope de Vega.

25. Fernando Lázaro Carreter, *Lope de Vega: Introducción a su vida y obra* (Salamanca: Ediciones Anaya, 1966), pp. 173–74. See especially his

pp. 169–78, subtitled "El teatro en Valencia." (The quotation from Gracián is found on p. 173.)

26. E. M. W. Tillyard, .The Elizabethan World Picture (New York: Random House Vintage Books, n.d.), p. 27.

27. Henry Bamford Parkes, The Divine Order: Western Culture in the Middle Ages and the Renaissance (New York: Alfred A. Knopf, 1969), p. 398, misses this point when he refers to Shakespeare's Othello: "When Othello becomes convinced of Desdemona's violation of her marriage vows, he immediately sees this as a threat to all ordered society, and the aspect of society which he chooses for emphasis is the glory of chivalric warfare." Parkes first suggests that perhaps Shakespeare was not fully aware of the implications of Othello's remarks (!), but then decides that the disruption of matrimony (although he generalizes too much by referring to "an act of unchastity") as "a denial of the whole social order" was indeed Othello's view "and it seems probable that it was also Shakespeare's."

28. Ibid., p. 64.

29. Philip Vellacott, translator, The Bacchae and Other Plays, by Euripides (Middlesex: Penguin Books Ltd., 1954), p. 30.

30. Euripides, Medea, translated by R. C. Trevelyan, in An Anthology of Greek Drama, ed. C. A. Robinson, Jr. (New York: Rinehart and Co., 1951), p. 147.

For a contrary view on vengeance, see Jenaro Artiles, "La idea de venganza en el drama español del siglo XVII," Segismundo, 3 (1967), 9–38. Artiles stresses primarily vengeance as a response to adultery, whereas the plays of the Valencians show vengeance to be important in nonsexual matters. Moreover, Artiles does give examples to show that while vengeance may indeed be considered unchristian at times (more often by moralists than by dramatists), there are sufficient occasions when vengeance is more important than justice.

31. I obviously agree with Margaret Wilson's conclusion of the importance of Seneca as an influence on the comedia, but as my text indicates, more significance attaches to the bloodshed and violence than a desire to portray horror on the stage. See her previously cited Spanish Drama of the Golden Age, p. 18: "Even on those few authors who took cognizance of the classical theatre, the chief influence was not that of the Greeks but of Seneca. His strain of horror, violence and bloodshed is strong in them, as in Thomas Kyd and the Elizabethans. It was to persist in later Spanish drama when Aristotelian forms were swept aside, and is the one clear legacy of the ancient theatre to the comedia."

Selected Bibliography

PRIMARY SOURCES

1. Manuscripts

Aguilar, Gaspar de. *El mercader amante.* MS. 17.334 in the Biblioteca
  Nacional de Madrid, from the early 17th century.

———. *Los amantes de Cartago.* Copy (16.018) in the Biblioteca Nacional
  de Madrid, from the 19th century.

Beneyto, Miguel de. *El hijo obediente.* MS. 18.074 in the Biblioteca Nacional de Madrid, from the first half of the 19th century.

Tárrega, Francisco Agustín. *El Prado de Valencia.* Copy (18.073) in the
  Biblioteca Nacional de Madrid, from the 19th century.

———. *La perseguida Amaltea.* Copy (18.074) in the Biblioteca Nacional de
  Madrid, from the 19th century.

———. *La sangre leal y descendencia de los reyes de Navarra.* MS. 4.117 in
  the Biblioteca Nacional de Madrid. The Paz y Melia Catalogue
  (*Catálogo de las piezas de teatro que se conservan en el Departamento
  de manuscritos de la Biblioteca Nacional,* 2nd ed., Madrid, 1934)
  mentions the variant title *La sangre real de los montañeses de Navarra.*
  Juliá, whose edition I have been following, evidently preferred the
  second title, although he changed the word *real* ("royal") to *leal* ("loyal"). Since the other version ties loyal blood to the descent of kings and
  the variant title ties royal blood to residents of the mountainous regions, there is room for further research with respect to Américo
  Castro's thesis that the *cristiano viejo* had his origins in such regions.

2. Early editions

*Doze comedias famosas de quatro poetas naturales de la insigne y coronada
  ciudad de Valencia.* Edited by Aurelio Mey. Valencia: Casa Iusepe
  Ferrer, 1608. Contains *comedias* by Tárrega, Aguilar, Castro, and
  Beneyto.

*Doze comedias famosas de quatro poetas naturales de la Insigne y Coronada
  Ciudad de Valencia.* Barcelona: Sebastián de Cormellas, 1609. Reprinting of the preceding entry.

157

Doze comedias famosas de quatro poetas naturales de la insigne y coronada ciudad de Valencia. Madrid: Miguel Martínez, 1616. Another reprinting of the 1608 edition, but as Juliá indicates in the commentary of his own edition (p. lxv), the 1614 edition contains lines that are missing in the 1609 edition and which exist in the 1608 edition.

Norte de la poesía española: Illustrado del sol de doze Comedias (que forman Segunda parte) de Laureados Poetas Valencianos: y de doze escogidas Loas, y otras Rimas a varios sugetos. Edited by Aurelio Mey. Valencia: Iusepe Ferrer, 1616. Contains plays by Tárrega, Aguilar, Turia, and Boil.

Rey de Artieda, Andrés. *Los amantes.* Valencia: Casa de la Viuda de Pedro de Huete, 1581. The only extant copy of this edition is in the Biblioteca Nacional de Madrid.

————. *Los amantes.* Valencia: Casa de Manuel Pau, 1908. Reprinting of the 1581 edition, but poorly done, as indicated in my note 19 to chapter 2. Only 51 copies were printed.

Virués, Cristóbal de. *Obras trágicas y líricas del Capitán Cristóbal de Virués.* Madrid: Estevan Bogia, 1609. Contains the five known *comedias* of Virués. Hermenegildo, in *La tragedia en el renacimiento español,* p. 586, shares the opinion of Salvá (Pedro Salvá y Mallén, *Catálogo de la biblioteca de Salvá,* Valencia, 1872) that there was an earlier edition, but no one has been able to document this.

3. Modern editions

Dramáticos contemporáneos a Lope de Vega. Edited by Ramón de Mesonero Romanos. Madrid: M. Rivadeneyra, 1857. *Biblioteca de Autores Españoles,* 43. Following an introduction which is somewhat outdated but still of interest, and in addition to works by Castro and six other dramatists of the time, the volume includes 4 *comedias* by Tárrega, 3 by Aguilar, 1 by Boil, and 1 by Turia.

Poetas dramáticos valencianos. Edited by Eduardo Juliá Martínez. 2 vols. Madrid: Real Academia Española, 1929. Following a detailed and highly important introduction of 135 pages, this edition presents all the known *comedias* by the Valencians discussed in the present study. Despite some errors which appear to be the fault of the printer rather than of the editor, this set constitutes the most valuable edition of the Valencian dramas.

Rey de· Artieda, Andrés. *Los amantes.* Edited by Agustín González de Amezúa. Madrid: La Arcadia, 1947.

Selección de comedias del Siglo de Oro español. Edited by Alva V. Ebersole. Madrid: Editorial Castalia, 1973. *Estudios de Hispanófila,* 24. Following a brief prologue and an appendix which includes Artieda's own prologue to *Los amantes,* Ebersole prefaces each author's *comedia* with a brief introduction to his works. In addition to *comedias* by Claramonte, Lope de Vega, Alarcón, Tirso, Mira de Amesuca, Vélez de Guevara and Calderón, the Valencians are represented by Tárrega's *El Prado de Valencia*, Virués' *La gran Semíramis*, and Castro's *El perfecto caballero*.

Virués, Cristóbal de. *La gran Semíramis*. Leipzig: n.p., 1858.

SECONDARY SOURCES

ALPERN, HYMEN. "Jealousy as a Dramatic Motive in the Spanish 'Comedia.'" *Romanic Review* 14 (1923), 276–85.

AMEZÚA, AGUSTÍN G. DE. *Cervantes, creador de la novela corta española*. 2 vols. Madrid: Consejo Superior de Investigaciones Científicas, 1956–58. One of the most extensive and detailed studies of Cervantes' *Novelas ejemplares*.

ARISTOTLE. *Poetics*. Translation © 1932 by S. H. Butcher, as reprinted in *Aristotle's Poetics*. New York: Hill and Wang, 1961. Quoted by permission of Macmillan Publishing Co., Inc., New York, and by permission of Macmillan, London and Basingstoke.

ASCHCOM, BENJAMIN B. "Concerning 'la mujer en hábito de hombre en la comedia.'" *Hispanic Review* 28 (1960), 43–62.

ATKINSON, WILLIAM C. "Séneca, Virués, Lope de Vega." In *Homenatge a Antoni Rubió i Lluch*. Barcelona: Estudis Universitaris Catalans, 1936, I, 111–31. Stresses the position of Virués as the link between Seneca and Lope. An important contribution but occasionally marred by generalizations.

AUBRUN, CHARLES V. *La comedia española*. Madrid: Taurus Ediciones, 1968. Translation by Julio Lago Alonso of the original French edition, *La Comédie espagnole* (Paris: Presses Universitaires de France, 1966). The purpose is to study the apogee of the *comedia* (1600–1680), which explains the absence of the Valencians, although I must quarrel with the classification of Guillén de Castro among the pioneers.

BARRERA Y LEIRADO, CAYETANO ALBERTO DE LA. *Catálogo bibliográfico y biográfico del teatro antiguo español, desde sus orígenes hasta mediados del siglo XVIII*. Madrid: M. Rivadeneyra, 1860. An alphabetically arranged "Who's Who" type of catalogue of Spanish dramatists through the first half of the eighteenth century.

BERSHAS, HENRY N. "The Source of Gaspar Aguilar's *La venganza honrosa*." *Romance Notes* 8 (1967), 266–69. Demonstrates that Aguilar anticipated Lope's use of epic and chronicle sources for the *comedia*.

BOMLI, R. W. *La Femme dans l'Espagne du siècle d'or*. La Haye: Martinus Nijhoff, 1950. A concise study of the treatment of women by Golden Age authors in Spain.

BRAVO-VILLASANTE, CARMEN. *La mujer vestida de hombre en el teatro español (siglos XVI–XVII)*. Madrid: Revista de Occidente, 1955.

CASALDUERO, JOAQUÍN. *Sentido y forma del Quijote.* Madrid: Ediciones Insula, 1949.

CASTRO, AMÉRICO. "Algunas observaciones acerca del concepto del honor en los siglos XVI y XVII." *Revista de Filología Española* 3 (1916), 1–50, 357–86. Somewhat outdated, as admitted by Castro himself, but an indispensable study to begin the comprehension of the nuances involved not only in the *comedia* but in other works as well.

————. *De la edad conflictiva: El drama de la honra en España y en su literatura.* Madrid: Taurus Ediciones, 1961. Despite the secondary title, the subject is not specifically the drama on the stage but the dramatic conflict brought about by the concept in real life as to what was honor, who had it, and how it could be lost or regained and in this sense, a natural subject for the theater. The concept of the *cristiano viejo* is studied in detail. No student of the Golden Age should fail to read critically this important contribution.

————. "La comedia clásica." In *El concepto contemporáneo de España.* Edited by Angel del Río and M. J. Benardete. Buenos Aires: Editorial Losada, 1946, pp. 591–610.

CASTRO, GUILLÉN DE. *Las mocedades del Cid.* Edited by Víctor Said Armesto. Madrid: Espasa-Calpe, 1952. *Clásicos Castellanos,* 15.

————. *Obras de don Guillén de Castro y Bellvis.* Ed. Eduardo Juliá Martínez. 3 vols. Madrid: Real Academia Española, 1925–27.

————. *The Youthful Deeds of the Cid.* New York: Exposition Press, 1969. Translation of *Las mocedades del Cid* by Robert R. La Du, Luis Soto-Ruiz, and Giles A. Daeger, with introduction by John G. Weiger. To my knowledge, this is unfortunately the only English rendition of any play by any of the Valencian dramatists of the Golden Age.

CICERO. *De Officiis.* Translated by Walter Miller. Cambridge: Harvard University Press, 1956.

COTARELO Y MORI, EMILIO. "La fundación de la Academia Española y su primer director, don Juan Manuel F. Pacheco, Marqués de Villena." *Boletín de la Real Academia Española* 1 (1914), 4–38.

————. *Sobre el origen y desarrollo de la leyenda de los amantes de Teruel.* Madrid: Revista de Archivos, Bibliotecas y Museos, 1907.

CRAWFORD, J. P. WICKERSHAM. *Spanish Drama Before Lope de Vega.* Philadelphia: University of Pennsylvania Press, 1967. A revised edition with a bibliographical supplement by Warren T. McCready. Although the references to the Valencians do not go beyond Artieda and Virués, the book is indispensable for a comprehension of the pre-Lopean theater.

DUNN, P. N. "Honour and the Christian Background in Calderón." In *Critical Essays on the Theatre of Calderón.* Edited by Bruce W. Wardropper. New York: New York University Press, 1965, pp. 24–60. A reprinting of Dunn's article in the *Bulletin of Hispanic Studies*

(1960) which gives a perceptive examination of the ethical significance of the honor code.

EBERSOLE, CARMEN I. DE. "Andrés Rey de Artieda *y Los amantes de Teruel.*" *Hispanófila* 41 (1971), 13–21. Demonstrates that the seeds planted by Artieda bore fruit in the later *comedia*.

EDWARDS, GWYNNE. "Calderón's *La hija del aire* in the Light of His Sources." *Bulletin of Hispanic Studies* 43 (1966), 177–96.

FLECNIAKOSKA, JEAN-LOUIS. "L'horreur morale et l'horreur matérielle dans quelques tragédies espagnoles du XVIᶜ siècle," in *Les tragédies de Sénèque et le théatre de la renaissance.* Paris: Editions du Centre National de la Recherche Scientifique, 1964.

FROLDI, RINALDO. *Lope de Vega y la formación de la comedia.* Salamanca: Ediciones Anaya, 1968. Revised edition, translation by Franco Gabriel of the Italian *Il teatro valenzano e l'origine della commedia barocca* (Pisa: Editrice Tecnico-Scientifica, 1962). The best work to date on the place of the Valencian culture, particularly the drama, in the evolution of the Spanish national *comedia*. Insists that the notion of Lope de Vega as the creator is a romantic and unscholarly posture. The Fall, 1974 issue of the *Bulletin of the Comediantes* lists this book in its bibliography section with a 1973 publication date. I have been unable to ascertain whether this is a reprinting or a new edition.

FUCILLA, JOSEPH G. Review of *Il teatro valenzano e l'origine della commedia barocca*, by Froldi. *Hispania* 47 (1964), 866–67.

GAGEN, JEAN. "Love and Honor in Dryden's Heroic Plays." *PMLA* 77 (1962), 208–20.

GASCÓN Y GUIMBAO, DOMINGO. *Los amantes de Teruel: Antonio Serón y su "Silva a Cintia."* Madrid: Imprenta de los Hijos de M. G. Hernández, 1907.

GONZÁLEZ-QUEVEDO, BENITO R. *Vida y obra dramática del canónigo Francisco Agustín Tárrega.* Unpublished dissertation at the University of North Carolina, Chapel Hill, 1971. I have not had an opportunity to examine this work.

GREEN, OTIS H. "Imaginative Authority in Spanish Literature." *PMLA* 84 (1969), 209–16. The presidential address delivered at the 83rd annual meeting of the MLA, which touches upon many of the points raised in my study and should be read by those interested in the ethical nature of Spanish literature.

———. *Spain and the Western Tradition.* 4 vols. Madison: The University of Wisconsin Press, 1963–66. A lifetime of erudition with particular emphasis on the relationship of literature and the history of ideas through the end of the Golden Age.

HERMENEGILDO, ALFREDO. *Los trágicos españoles del siglo XVI.* Madrid: Fundación Universitaria Española, 1961. A voluminous examination of potential tragedies in Spain during the sixteenth century. Artieda and

Virués are analyzed at length but the insistence on seeing tragedy in its conventional sense is at times forced.

———. *La tragedia en el renacimiento español.* Barcelona: Editorial Planeta, 1973. A revised edition of the work described in the preceding entry. It is updated in many respects but some entire sections are verbatim repetitions of the 1961 book.

———. "Adulación, ambición e intriga: los cortesanos de la primitiva tragedia española." Article as yet unpublished but summarized in *La tragedia en el renacimiento español*, and which promises to shed more light on Virués' portrayal of women as virile and unscrupulous.

HESSE, EVERETT W. and VALENCIA, JUAN O. *El teatro anterior a Lope de Vega.* Madrid: Ediciones Alcalá, 1971. *Colección Aula Magna*, 23.

JULIÁ MARTÍNEZ, EDUARDO. *Lope de Vega y Valencia.* Madrid: C. Bermejo, 1935. Deals with Lope's visit to Valencia.

———. "Nuevos datos sobre Micer Andrés Rey de Artieda." *Boletín de la Real Academia Española* 20 (1933), 667–86.

———. Review of *Il teatro valenzano e l'origine della commedia barocca*, by Froldi. *Revista de Literatura* 21 (1962), 181–83.

KENNEDY, RUTH LEE. "A Reappraisal of Tirso's Relations to Lope and His Theatre." *Bulletin of the Comediantes* 17 (1965), 23–34.

KLEIN, J. L. *Geschichte des Spanischen Dramas.* 4 vols. Leipzig: T. O. Weigel, 1871–75.

LA DU, ROBERT R. "Honor and the King in the *Comedias* of Guillén de Castro." *Hispania* 45 (1962), 211–17. A significant investigation of the honor concept as developed by Castro, useful for comparison with the Valencians in general.

LÁZARO CARRETER, FERNANDO. *Lope de Vega: Introducción a su vida y obra.* Salamanca: Ediciones Anaya, 1966. The section entitled "El teatro en Valencia," on pp. 169–78, supports the importance of the Valencian theater prior to Lope.

LEAVITT, STURGIS E. *An Introduction to Golden Age Drama in Spain.* Madrid: Editorial Castalia, 1971. *Estudios de Hispanófila*, 19.

———. "Spanish *Comedias* as Pot Boilers." *PMLA* 82 (1967), 181–83. Reveals the necessity of dramatists and actors alike to make a living in addition to creating art.

LEFEBVRE, ALFREDO. *La fama en el teatro de Lope.* Madrid: Taurus Ediciones, 1962. An interesting brief analysis which does see the connection between honor and virtuous actions. Unfortunately, the initial page promises to deal with a large number of Lope's plays but the author limits himself to dealing with only ten. The major emphasis lies in an exposition of how characters in Lope's plays may enhance their *fama*.

LÓPEZ MORALES, HUMBERTO. *Tradición y creación en los orígenes del teatro castellano.* Madrid: Ediciones Alcalá, 1968.

MANRIQUE, JORGE. "Coplas por la muerte de su padre." In vol. II of

Cancionero castellano del siglo XV. Nueva biblioteca de autores españoles, 21 (Madrid, 1915). Other Spanish editions are readily found in anthologies. Two which are accompanied by footnotes in English are Walter T. Pattison, *Representative Spanish Authors*, 2nd edition (New York: Oxford University Press, 1958), I, 34–40; and Richard E. Chandler and Kessel Schwartz, *A New Anthology of Spanish Literature* (Baton Rouge: Louisiana State University Press, 1967), I, 268–74. A prose translation titled "Verses on the Death of His Father" appears in *The Penguin Book of Spanish Verse*, ed. J. M. Cohen (Middlesex: Penguin Books Ltd., 1956), pp. 40–59, which is probably the most accessible version in English. See also Longfellow's translation in *Ten Centuries of Spanish Poetry*, ed. Eleanor L. Turnbull (Baltimore: Grove Press, 1955).

MARTÍ GRAJALES, FRANCISCO. *Ensayo de un diccionario biográfico y bibliográfico de los poetas que florecieron en el reino de Valencia hasta el año 1700*. Madrid: Revista de Archivos, Bibliotecas y Museos, 1927. Similar in format to the Barrera volume cited above, but more recent and confined to Valencia.

MÉRIMÉE, HENRI. *L'Art dramatique à Valencia* Toulouse: Librairie Edouard Privat, 1913. Until the appearance of the works by Juliá and Froldi, the standard work on the Valencian drama. Still of importance and filled with data, the major reservation deals with impressionistic interpretations (although this is not always the case).

———. "Sur la biographie de Gaspar Aguilar." *Bulletin Hispanique* 9 (1906), 393–96.

MONTOLIU, MANUEL DE. *El alma de España y sus reflejos en la literatura del Siglo de Oro*. Barcelona: Editorial Cervantes, n.d.

MORBY, EDWIN S. Review of *Il teatro valenzano e l'origine della commedia barocca*, by Froldi. *Hispanic Review* 32 (1964), 265–68.

MORLEY, S. GRISWOLD. "Strophes in the Spanish Drama Before Lope de Vega." In *Homenaje ofrecido a Menéndez Pidal: Miscelánea de estudios lingüísticos, literarios e históricos*, vol. I (Madrid: Librería Hernando, 1925), pp. 505–31.

NORTHUP, GEORGE T. *Three Plays by Calderón*. Boston: D. C. Heath, 1926. Despite the passage of more than half a century, the introduction is still one of the most valuable essays on Calderón, particularly with respect to the honor code.

ORDUNA, GERMÁN. "Las *Coplas* de Jorge Manrique y el triunfo sobre la muerte: Estructura e intencionalidad." *Romanische Forschungen* 79 (1967), 139–51.

PARKER, A. A. *The Approach to the Spanish Drama of the Golden Age*. London: The Hispanic and Luso-Brazilian Councils, 1957. One of the most fundamental studies of the essence of the *comedia*, despite its brevity.

PARKES, HENRY BAMFORD. *The Divine Order: Western Culture in the*

Middle Ages and the Renaissance. New York: Alfred A. Knopf, 1969. A very readable account of the development of cultural traditions from the Dark and Middle Ages to the Renaissance.

PARTRIDGE, ERIC. *Origins: A Short Etymological Dictionary of Modern English.* New York: The Macmillan Co., 1959.

PÉREZ DE GUZMÁN, JUAN. "Academias literarias de ingenios y señores bajo los Austrias." *La España Moderna* 6 (1894), 68–107.

PFANDL, LUDWIG. *Cultura y costumbres del pueblo español de los siglos XVI y XVII: Introducción al estudio del Siglo de Oro.* Barcelona: Casa Editorial Araluce, 1929.

PRING-MILL, R. D. F. "Sententiousness in *Fuente Ovejuna.*" *Tulane Drama Review* 7 (1962), 5–37. A stimulating analysis to show that the *comedia* used aphorisms to reveal general truths while apparently referring to the immediate scene in question.

REICHENBERGER, ARNOLD G. "The Uniqueness of the *Comedia.*" *Hispanic Review* 27 (1959), 303–16. One of the most oft-quoted studies of the *comedia.* The major conclusion, that the *comedia* rests on the two pillars of honor and faith, is restated in the 1970 article by the same title, adding love as a major element but spending too much time on defending himself against the criticism expressed by Eric Bentley in the latter's "The Universality of the *Comedia,*" *Hispanic Review* 38 (1970), 147–62.

RENNERT, HUGO A. *The Spanish Stage in the Time of Lope de Vega.* New York: Hispanic Society of America, 1909.

ROGERS, DANIEL. "'¡Cielos! ¿Quién en Ninias habla?': The Mother-Son Impersonation in *La hija del aire.*" *Bulletin of the Comediantes* 20 (1968), 1–4.

ROMERA NAVARRO, M. "Las disfrazadas de varón en la comedia" *Hispanic Review* 2 (1934), 269–86.

ROTHBERG, IRVING P. "El agente cómico de Lope de Vega." *Hispanófila* 16 (1962), 69–90. Discusses many elements of comedy, including the possession of a character's "comic flaw."

RUIZ RAMÓN, FRANCISCO. *Historia del teatro español.* 2 vols. Madrid: Alianza Editorial, 1971.

SALVÁ, PEDRO, ed. *Cancionero de la Academia de los Nocturnos de Valencia.* 4 vols. Valencia: Imprenta de Francisco Vives Mora, 1905–12. Reedited with additions and notes by Martí Grajales. Includes biographical data but more importantly constitutes the collection of poems, speeches and other literary presentations made at the meetings by the members of the academy.

SÁNCHEZ, JOSÉ. *Academias literarias del Siglo de Oro español.* Madrid: Editorial Gredos, 1961. The most up-to-date source of information on the literary academies that flourished in Madrid, Seville, Valencia, Aragón, and elsewhere during the Golden Age.

SARGENT, CECILIA VENNARD. *A Study of the Dramatic Works of Cristóbal de Virués*. New York: Instituto de las Españas, 1930. Thus far, the only book-length study of any of the dramatists analyzed in the present book. Miss Sargent's book was to have served as an introduction to an annotated edition of the dramas of Virués, but the appearance of Juliá's edition of the Valencian dramas forced the Sargent work to limit itself to the critical, biographical, and bibliographical study it became.

SCHAEFFER, ADOLF. *Geschichte des Spanischen Nationaldramas*. 2 vols. Leipzig: F. A. Brockhaus, 1890.

SENECA. *The Stoic Philosophy of Seneca*. Essays and Letters translated by Moses Hadas. Garden City: Doubleday Anchor Books, 1958.

SERRANO CAÑETE, JOAQUÍN. *El canónigo Francisco-Agustín Tárrega: Estudio biográfico bibliográfico*. Valencia: José Ortega, 1889. Originally a lecture read on May 25, 1889, and subsequently published.

TILLYARD, E. M. W. *The Elizabethan World Picture*. New York: Random House Vintage Books, n.d. A concise study of the Renaissance views of the universe, particularly with regard to "the great chain of being."

VALBUENA BRIONES, ÁNGEL. *Perspectiva crítica de los dramas de Calderón*. Madrid: Ediciones Rialp, 1965.

VALBUENA PRAT, ÁNGEL. *El teatro español en su Siglo de Oro*. Barcelona: Editorial Planeta, 1969.

_____. *Historia de la literatura española*. 3 vols. Barcelona: Editorial Gili, 1964.

_____. *Literatura dramática española*. Barcelona: Editorial Labor, 1950.

VEGA, LOPE DE. "The New Art of Writing Plays." Translation of *El arte nuevo de hacer comedias en este tiempo* by William T. Brewster, with an introduction by Brander Matthews, in *Papers on Playmaking* (New York: Hill and Wang, 1957), pp. 1–19. There exist many editions in Spanish. I highly recommend the volume edited by Juana de José Prades, published by the Consejo Superior de Investigaciones Científicas (Madrid, 1971), which includes a reproduction of the Madrid edition of 1613 and provides a line by line analysis. The preliminary study also makes mention of the fact that the first to write a laudatory poem about Lope's verses, which were published in Seville in 1604, was Virués.

VOSSLER, CARLOS [KARL]. *Lope de Vega y su tiempo*. Madrid: Revista de Occidente, 1940.

WADE, GERALD E. " 'El burlador de Sevilla': Some Annotations." *Hispania* 47 (1964), 751–61.

_____. "La comicidad de 'Don Gil de las calzas verdes' de Tirso de Molina." *Revista de Archivos, Bibliotecas y Museos* 76 (1973), 475–86. An important attempt to see the comic nature of a character in ethical and societal terms.

_____. Review of *La Comedia y sus intérpretes*, by Everett W. Hesse. *Bulletin of the Comediantes* 26 (1974), 35–36.

WARDROPPER, BRUCE W. "Lope's *La dama boba* and Baroque Comedy."

Bulletin of the Comediantes 13 (1961), 1–3. An interesting attempt to demonstrate the comic nature of problems encountered prior to marriage as a preparation for the more serious future.

WATSON, CURTIS BROWN. *Shakespeare and the Renaissance Concept of Honor.* Princeton: Princeton University Press, 1960. The first part is an inclusive study of the evolution of the honor concept from Plato to the Renaissance and is highly recommended for anyone wishing a coherent and well-written survey of the history of an idea. The second part examines how this concept was applied by Shakespeare to his drama.

WEIGER, JOHN G. "Nobility in the Theater of Virués." *Romance Notes* 7 (1966), 180–82. Attempts to demonstrate that bandits in *La infelice Marcela* are of noble and possibly royal ancestry, which would explain their behavior and language.

————. "Sobre la originalidad e independencia de Guillén de Castro." *Hispanófila* 31 (1967), 1–15. Attempts to show that Castro's talent lay in his ability to adapt themes from epics, ballads, history, fiction, and his own imagination to Lope's format. While praising this talent, the article implicitly denies Castro the position of leader of a Valencian school, hence adds weight to the argument that the group did not represent a school.

————. "Tirso's Contribution in *Los amantes de Teruel.*" *Bulletin of the Comediantes* 19 (1967), 33–35. Discusses Tirso de Molina's use of the legend and how he adapted it to the *comedia* of the seventeenth century.

————. Review of *Guillén de Castro*, by William E. Wilson. *Bulletin of the Comediantes* 26 (1974), 82–84.

WILLIAMSEN, VERN G. Review of *An Introduction to Golden Age Drama in Spain*, by Sturgis E. Leavitt. *Hispania* 57 (1974), 597–98. This review implicitly demonstrates the need to study *comedias* other than those typically taught in survey classes. Williamsen points out that the plays chosen by Leavitt "are those traditionally presented (too frequently one might be led to comment) in the introductory *comedia* course. He says little that is new about any. In fact, he repeats many of the canards that have become the butt of modern criticism" (p. 597).

WILSON, MARGARET. *Spanish Drama of the Golden Age.* Oxford: Pergamon Press Ltd., 1969.

WILSON, WILLIAM E. *Guillén de Castro.* New York: Twayne Publishers, Inc., 1973. Twayne's World Authors Series, 253.

WOOD, NEAL. "Some Common Aspects of the Thought of Seneca and Machiavelli." *Renaissance Quarterly* 21 (1968), 11–23. Discusses the etymological development of the Latin *virtus*, which even Seneca understood in military terms.

YAGÜE DE SALAS, JUAN. *Los amantes de Teruel: epopeya trágica.* Teruel: Instituto de Estudios Turolenses, 1951.

Index